nitty gritty books

Seafoods Cookbook
Quick Breads
Pasta & Rice
Calorie Watchers Cookbook
Pies & Cakes
Yogurt
The Ground Beef Cookbook
Cocktails & Hors d'Oeuvres
Casseroles & Salads
Kid's Party Book
Pressure Cooking
Food Processor Cookbook
Peanuts & Popcorn
Kid's Pets Book
Make It Ahead French Cooking

Soups & Stews
Crepes & Omelets
Microwave Cooking
Vegetable Cookbook
Kid's Arts and Crafts
Bread Baking
The Crockery Pot Cookbook
Kid's Garden Book
Classic Greek Cooking
Low Carbohydrate Cookbook
Kid's Cookbook
Italian
Cheese Guide & Cookbook
Miller's German
Quiche & Souffle

To My Daughter, With Love
Natural Foods
Chinese Vegetarian
The Jewish Cookbook
Working Couples
Mexican
Sunday Breakfast
Fisherman's Wharf Cookbook
Barbecue Cookbook
Ice Cream Cookbook
Blender Cookbook
The Wok, a Chinese Cookbook
Japanese Country
Fondue Cookbook

designed with giving in mind

To all my friends ocean to ocean who contributed recipes; to the New Jersey fishermen and fishmongers who assisted with seafood information; to Dave, Kathy and Kristy, who had fish for dinner every night for months; and, finally, to Tom, who always saw to it there were no leftovers.

With deepest thanks,
Sally Morris
Middletown, New Jersey

Seafood

by
Sally Murphy Morris

Illustrated by Mike Nelson
Edited by Maureen Reynolds

©Copyright 1979
Nitty Gritty Productions
Concord, California

A Nitty Gritty Book*
Published by
Nitty Gritty Productions
P.O. Box 5457
Concord, California 94524

*Nitty Gritty Books — Trademark
Owned by Nitty Gritty Productions
Concord, California

ISBN 0-911954-52-X
Library of Congress Catalog Card Number: 79-2433

TABLE OF CONTENTS

INTRODUCTION

When well-intentioned shoppers venture to their local markets, intent upon buying seafood, they are often faced with a mind-boggling array.

Shopping for seafood can be a marvelous adventure, when you're equipped with enthusiasm and the proper knowledge. However, enthusiasm alone is not enough for the novice of seafood cookery. Before you can visit the fish market with confidence, a few basic pieces of knowledge are essential.

Although your questions and problems may seem insurmountable at first, many of them may be answered in the same way. For example, you may be intimidated by the multitude of species of seafood. With over 25,000 classified varieties of fin and shellfish, it's no wonder. "How," you may ask, "am I going to remember the names?" Although this may seem like the solution at first, it simply is not conceivable, or useful, to memorize the names of all edible seafoods. The substitutions chart, beginning on page 25, lists the families and individual names of most edible fish. Become familiar with the fish families and their characteristics. The next time you visit your fish market, bring the chart with you. That way you can see the fish as you read about them. To familiarize yourself with shellfish, read ABOUT SHELLFISH, on page 34.

Another problem you may encounter is market labeling. The label a fish bears is not always indicative of the family to which it belongs. For example, a white perch is not a member of the perch family, but a member of the bass family. By checking the substitutions chart, you will be able to ascertain the family to which a fish belongs.

Availability may pose another problem. Nothing is more frustrating than being unable to locate a particular seafood, once you've chosen a recipe. Fortunately, almost any fish can be substituted with another of similar fat content, flavor and texture. Once again, the chart on page 25 will help you determine which fish are interchangeable.

After you feel comfortable with the substitutions chart and the introductory sections on shellfish, you will be equipped with enough knowledge to begin to meet the challenges of seafood cookery. Detailed instructions, complete with illustrations, will guide you through the selection and preparation process of seafood cookery. You'll learn how to dress a fish, shuck an oyster and more. Last, but not least, a delectable array of kitchen-tested recipes, gathered from around the country, will culminate your initiation into the world of seafood cookery.

Consumption of seafoods has expanded 60% in the last 11 years, so join the crowd!

THE "HOW TO'S"
OF SELECTING AND PREPARING FISH

How to Judge Freshness

Before you buy fish, check it closely. Don't buy it if it can't pass these tests:

Eyes   Clear, bright and bulging. Old fish have sunken, cloudy eyes.
Gills   Red, free of slime and odor. Old fish are gray, then brown, then green.
Scales   Tightly adhered to skin with a marked sheen.
Flesh   firm, elastic, springs back when touched. Old skin is dry and browned.
Odor   Fresh, not objectionable.

How Much Fish to Buy

Because appetites vary greatly, this is strictly a guide.

Whole or round	1 lb. per serving
Dressed	1/2 lb. per serving
Steaks, fillets, sticks	1/3 lb. per serving

Fish Forms Prior to Cooking

Become familiar with these common fish forms, whether you are shopping, cooking or even going out to dinner.

Whole or Round:

This is the least expensive form of fish, although only 45% of it is edible. This is the fish just as it comes from the water.

Drawn or Cleaned:

This is the whole fish with entrails (innards) removed. It is about 48% edible.

Dressed:

This is the whole fish with entrails, scales and fins removed. Sometimes the tail and/or head have been removed. It is about 67% edible.

Steaks and Chunks:

These are cross sections of fish with only a small piece of bone in each section. Fish steaks are usually 1-inch thick. Fish chunks are usually 4 to 6 inches in diameter. These forms are about 84% edible.

Fillets:

These are meaty slices of fish, cut lengthwise from just behind the head to the tail. They are nearly boneless and may be skinless. They are almost 100% edible.

Butterfly:

This is a double fillet, with the two sides connected at the backbone. It is nearly boneless. Because fish is not usually marketed in this form, you'll probably have to specially order it from your fishmonger. A butterfly fillet is almost 100% edible.

Fingers:

These are 1/2-inch wide strips, cut vertically, against the grain of fish fillets. They are usually sold frozen in a breading. They are 100% edible.

Sticks or Portions:

These are large (about 3 inches by 7 inches), rectangular strips of fish, cut from commercially frozen blocks of fillets. They too are usually sold frozen in a breading. They are 100% edible.

How to Store Fish

Fish deteriorates rapidly. The process begins as soon as it leaves the water, so handling fish with care is important. If you are catching your own, put it on ice immediately. If you purchase it at the market, return home as quickly as possible. When you arrive home, treat the fish in one of the following ways:

1. If you are not planning on eating the fish within 2 days, freeze it. The proper procedure for this is first to dress the fish (see page 8). Second, wrap the fish in plastic bags. Third, wrap the fish again using freezer paper. Date and label your fish. Store it no more than 1 month. Avoid freezing fish whenever possible. Freezing robs fish of its delicate taste and texture, oftentimes.

2. If you plan on eating your fish within 2 days, dress it (see page 8), wrap it well, and store it in the coolest part of your refrigerator.

How to Prepare Fish for Cooking

If you don't plan on catching your own, you'll probably never have to clean a fish. Your fishmonger will do it for you. But, if you like to fish or have a friend who sometimes gives you fresh fish, you'll need to know the proper procedure.

You should have: A 6-inch fillet knife, a large cutting board, a fish scaler or spoon and some old newspapers.

Scaling:

Because fish scales have a tendency to "fly" all over the kitchen, some people prefer to scale their fish outside. Whether you do it outside or inside, follow these steps. First, soak the fish in salt water for five minutes. This makes scaling easier. Then place wet fish on cutting board. Keep newspaper spread out, so that you can put the scales in it as they collect. Hold the fish tail in your left hand. Pick up the scaler or spoon with your right hand. Then, beginning at the tail, carefully scrape toward the head to remove the scales. Make sure all scales are removed.

Dressing:

Also known as cleaning, gutting or drawing. To remove the entrails, make a belly cut from the anal or ventral fin to the pelvic fin.

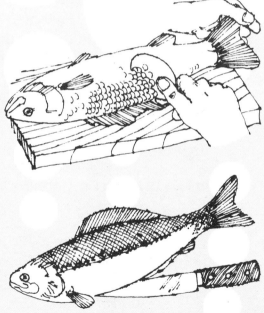

8

On a large fish, make a second cut from gill to gill, across the throat.

Using the point of your knife, pull out and discard the internal organs.

Unless your fish is very small and you plan to pan fry it, cut off the tail.

Remove the head, but don't throw it away! Save it for fish stock (see page 132).

Remove pectoral fins by cutting behind the gills and collarbone.

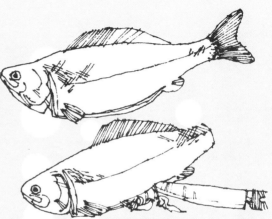

Remove the backbone by cutting on each side of the dorsal fin.

Pull the fin toward head. It should come out. If your fish is large, you may have to use a coping saw or cleaver to sever the backbone before it can be removed.

Remove the remaining fins by making an incision (a cut) around each. Pull them free. Rinse to remove any blood.

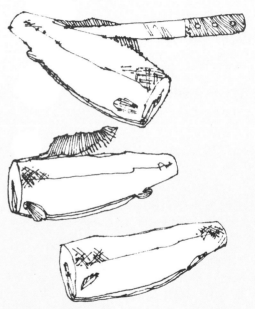

Your fish is now dressed. You may continue to operate on it, or cook it whole. If you wish to fillet, skin or cut your fish into steaks, follow these steps.

Filleting:

You may fillet fish without cleaning it. But, if the skin is to be left on, it must be scaled and gilled. To fillet, place fish on cutting board with belly side of fish closest to your body. With a fillet knife, make an incision just behind the pectoral fin. Slide the knife along the rib cage, from head to tail, using a sawing motion. The fillet should come off in one piece. Turn the fish over and repeat.

Skinning:

To skin the fish, work the knife between the flesh and the skin at the tail. While holding the tail in your left hand, pull the skin against the knife and draw knife away from tail. Save all scraps for stock (see page 132).

11

Filleting Flatfish:

Due to their large size and nearly flat shape, special instructions are needed to fillet flatfish. They require two horizontal cuts. Cut down to backbone, behind the head (cut 1). With the knife almost horizontal, slide it along the rib cage from the nape to the tail (cut 2). Repeat on other side. This should release the bones.

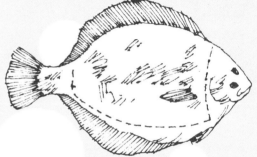

Cutting Steaks:

Cut 1-inch cross sections of dressed fish by slicing down through backbone with a heavy knife or cleaver. If the backbone is thick, either tap the knife with a mallet, or use a coping saw.

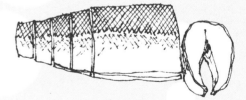

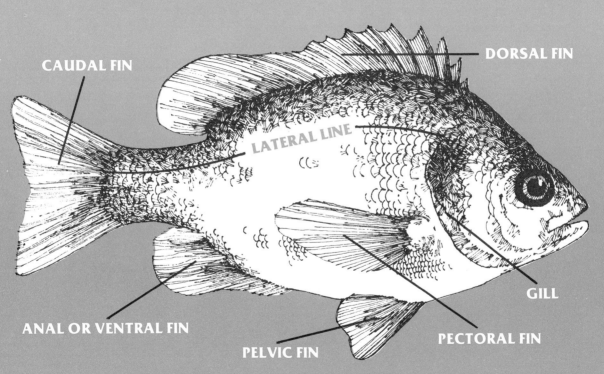

CAUDAL FIN

DORSAL FIN

LATERAL LINE

ANAL OR VENTRAL FIN

PELVIC FIN

GILL

PECTORAL FIN

13

BASIC WAYS OF COOKING FISH

DON'T OVERCOOK! This is the most important advice to be given about the cooking of fish. Excess cooking will only dry out and toughen the fish, making it rubbery and flavorless. Unlike many meats, fish is naturally tender. It should be cooked just to firm the flesh. Fish is done if it flakes when prodded with a fork.

Know the properties of your fish before you cook it. Ask your fishmonger or read over the description of your fish on the FISH FAMILIES Chart beginning on page 25. When you have identified whether your fish is lean or fatty and mild or strong in flavor, you are ready to choose the proper way to cook it. For instance, lean fish with less than 5% fat will need to be basted often to prevent drying out, especially if it is to be fried or baked. Fish with over 5% fat might need basting at the beginning of the cooking process, but may not need any further attention.

There are many different ways to cook fish, as you will see when you read this section. Choose the cooking method that is best suited to the type of fish you are using.

One more hint: Serve your fish immediately.

BAKING

Cleaned, dressed fish, whole steaks and fillets bake well. The flavor of a baked, whole fish is improved when the head and tail are left on. If you plan on stuffing the fish, fill it only 2/3 full, to allow for expansion. For easy clean-up, line the bottom of the pan with buttered brown paper or foil.

Basic Baked Fish

one 3 to 4 lb. fish, dressed
1/4 cup melted butter or margarine
salt and pepper to taste

Place fish in greased baking dish. Sprinkle inside and out with salt and pepper. Bake at 400°F. for 40 minutes, or until fish flakes. Baste twice during baking time with drippings. Makes 4 to 6 servings.

BROILING

Thick pieces of fish are best for broiling. Fillets don't work well because they dry out during the broiling process. You may marinate fish prior to broiling. Remember, lean fish must be basted often. For very thin fish, broil two inches from the heat source. For thick fish, broil four to six inches from heat source.

Basic Broiled Fish

2 lbs. fish steaks
2 tbs. melted butter **or** oil
2 tbs. lemon juice
1 tsp. salt
1/2 tsp. paprika
dash pepper

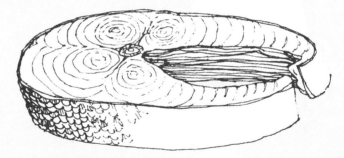

Place steaks in a single layer, on a preheated and greased broiler pan. Combine remaining ingredients. Pour over fish. Broil 4 to 6 minutes. Turn. Baste with sauce. Broil until fish flakes, 4 to 5 more minutes. Makes 6 servings.

OVEN FRYING

Once known as baking at a high temperature, this method is now called oven frying. It is a favorite because it renders a crisp fish without the odor, calories or clean-up of deep fat frying. It is faster than baking and very easy. The best pieces to use are: whole fish, dressed, fillets, or steaks. Cook 10 minutes for each inch of thickness: one inch thick = 10 minutes of cooking time; two inches thick = 20 minutes of cooking time. You do not have to turn the fish with this method of cooking.

Basic Oven Fried Fish

2 lbs. fish fillets
1 tbs. salt
1 cup milk

1 cup dry bread crumbs **or** cracker crumbs
1/4 cup melted butter **or** margarine

Cut fillets into serving sized portions. Add salt to milk. Dip fillets into milk, then into crumbs. Place in single layer in a greased baking dish. Drizzle butter evenly over top. Bake at 500°F. for about 10 minutes, or until fish flakes. Baste lean fish after 5 minutes. Makes 4 to 6 servings.

PAN FRYING

Small, whole fish, fillets and frozen fish portions or sticks are best prepared this way. Use oil in combination with butter to help prevent butter from burning. Fish prepared by pan frying will be crisp on the outside, tender and juicy on the inside.

Basic Pan Fried Fish

2 lbs. fillets, steaks or pan dressed fish
salt and pepper to taste
1 egg, beaten
1 tbs. milk
1 cup dry bread crumbs, cracker crumbs, cornmeal **or** flour
1/4 cup **each** butter and oil

Cut fillets into serving size pieces. Sprinkle both sides with salt and pepper. Add milk to egg, beat well. Dip fish in liquid mixture. Roll in crumbs. Melt butter with oil in large frying pan. Fry fish over moderate heat until brown on one side. Turn, brown on other side. Remove when fish flakes. Drain on absorbent paper. Makes 4 servings.

DEEP FAT FRYING

Small fish fillets are best for this method. Before you dip the fish in batter, the fish must be completely dry, or else the batter will not stick. Use a deep fat fryer, wok, or deep, heavy pan. Fill it only half full with vegetable oil. The oil must be hot enough, usually 375ºF., or the fish will be greasy. It is wise to use a thermometer. Make sure you use only fresh oil. Cook only a few pieces of fish at a time, so that temperature of oil will not drop.

Basic Deep Fat Fried Fish

1/3 lb. small fish fillets, per serving
any fritter batter
vegetable **or** peanut oil, enough to half fill the pan
Mustard Sauce, page 163 (optional)

Cut fish into one-inch pieces. Dry them well. Dip in batter. Fry in oil heated to 375ºF., in heavy skillet, for 5 to 8 minutes. If desired, serve with Mustard Sauce.

POACHING

This method works with any type of fish. It is best, however, with whole, lean fish. Flavorful fish, such as salmon and red snapper, can be poached in lightly salted water. The flavor of mild fish is enhanced with the addition of herbs and spices to the poaching liquid. Some flavorful broths in which fish can be poached are Court

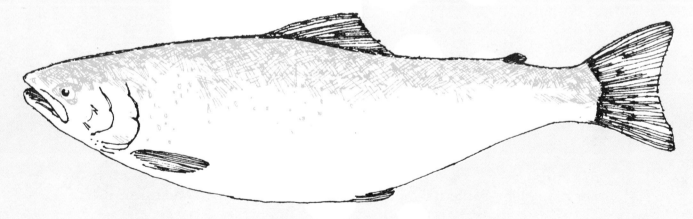

Bouillon (page 133) and Fish Stock (page 132). Unless you are using a fish poacher, wrap the fish in cheesecloth and lower it into liquid which just covers the fish. Simmer liquid 10 minutes for each inch of thickness of flesh. The cheesecloth will allow you to easily remove the fish intact from the liquid, when the fish is done. Reserve the broth accumulated in the pan for soups, sauces, or any recipe calling for fish stock.

Basic Poached Fish

2 lbs. fish fillets or steaks
cheesecloth (if not using fish poacher)
2 tsp. salt

Wrap fish in cheesecloth (if not using fish poacher). Place fish in single layer in poacher or large pan. Add enough water just to cover fish. Add salt. Bring to a boil over medium heat. Turn down heat to a low simmer. Cook until fish flakes, about 5 to 10 minutes. Makes 4 to 6 servings.

STEAMING

This is an excellent way to cook fillets, steaks or pan dressed fish without shrinkage. It will preserve the natural juices of the fish. Best of all, it is very low in calories.

Basic Steamed Fish

water or Court Bouillon, page 133
1/2 lb. fish fillets, per serving
salt and pepper to taste
cheesecloth

Pour liquid into pan or fish steamer. It should be an inch in depth. Bring liquid to a boil. Wrap fish in cheesecloth. Place fish in steamer, or on perforated tray above liquid. Cover. Steam for 5 to 10 minutes, depending upon the thickness of the fish. Save the liquid for making sauce.

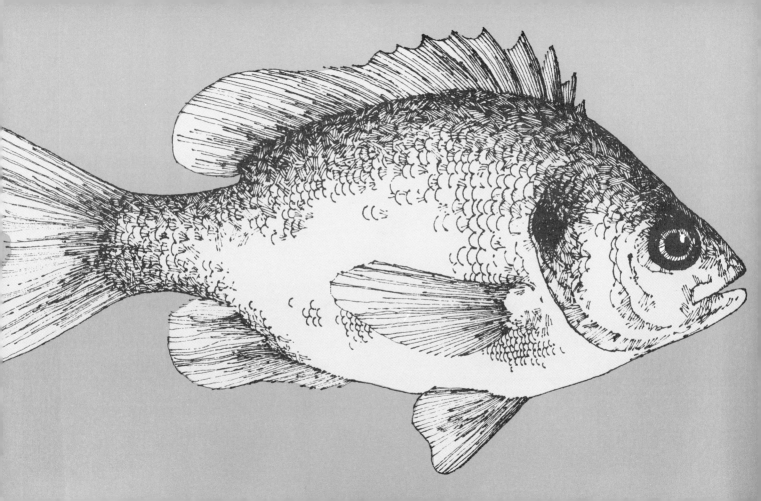

SUBSTITUTIONS

If you find a recipe you'd like to try, but the fish called for is unavailable, read over the chart beginning on page 25 for some alternatives. By comparing the descriptions of FISH FAMILIES, you should be able to find acceptable substitutes. The major factor to keep in mind is fat content. If your recipe calls for a lean fish, such as bass, substitute another lean fish, such as cod or perch. If an oily fish is called for, like catfish, substitute another oily fish, like mackerel.

When you become proficient in your understanding of fish, you may wish to interchange oily and lean fish. Remember, however, that a lean fish requires frequent basting.

If you have a fish of unknown fat content, check the flesh color. White, or very light colored fish is lean. Dark colored flesh indicates a high oil content. Tan, or light brown flesh indicates moderately fatty fish.

You'll find recipes for just about any fish imaginable, listed in the recipe index, beginning on page 174. Just look up your fish by name or family. For example: King Salmon is listed both under "K" and "S."

Fish Families	Flavor, Texture, Fat Content and Hints	Species
Bass	Mild flavor, Firm flesh. Low fat content. Remove leathery skin before cooking.	black bass, blackfish, black jewfish, black sea bass, crappie, giant sea bass, grouper, white sea bass, snook, striped bass, yellow bass, white perch
Bluefish	Depends upon where fish feeds. If Gulf Coast, sweet flavor, moderate fat content. If East Coast, strong flavor, high oil content.	blue snapper, fatback, skipjack, snapping macerel, tailor

Fish Families	Flavor, Texture, Fat Content and Hints	Species
Carp	Moderately strong flavor. Best in winter months. Firm flesh. Moderate fat content. Best cooked simply.	Bohemian/French, Israeli
Catfish	Delicate flavor. Firm, yet flaky. Moderate fat content. Remove leathery skin before eating. Good pan fried.	blue catfish, brown catfish, channel catfish, flat bullhead, gafftopsail, green bullhead, sea catfish, spotted catfish, walking catfish
Cod	Mild flavor. Tender flesh. Very low fat content.	Atlantic cod, burbot, codfish, cusk, hake, haddock, Pacific cod, pollock, poor cod, scrod, tomcod

Fish Families	Flavor, Texture, Fat Content and Hints	Species
Drum	Mild flavor. Tender flesh. Low fat content.	barbed drum, big drum, channel bass, croaker, drumfish, gray drum, sheepshead, striped drum white perch, whiting
Flounder	Mild, distinctive flavor. Tender, flaky flesh. Broiling not recommended because of low fat content.	American plaice, Atlantic halibut, arrowtooth, California halibut, fluke, Pacific halibut, sanddab, Southern flounder, starry flounder, turbot, windowpane

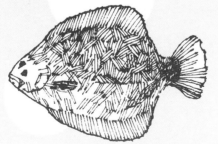

Fish Families	Flavor, Texture, Fat Content and Hints	Species
Mackerel	Rich, sometimes strong flavor. Firm flesh. High fat content. Before cooking remove dark lateral line of accumulated carbohydrates to avoid bitter taste.	American mackerel, Atlantic mackerel, bluefin, blue mackerel, bonita, Boston mackerel, Pacific mackerel, Spanish mackerel, tuna (albacore), yellowfin
Mullet	Mild flavor. Tender flesh. Moderate fat content.	black mullet, jumping mullet, liza, sand mullet, silver mullet, striped mullet, white mullet
Perch	Mild flavor. Tender, flaky flesh. Very low fat content. Small fish best pan fried.	blue pike, red perch, redfish, sauger, walleye, yellow perch, yellow pike

Fish Families	Flavor, Texture, Fat Content and Hints	Species
Pike	Mild flavor. Very bony. Low fat content. Difficult to scale. Pour boiling water over skin to ease job.	Muskelung, northern pike
Pompano	Rich, distinctive flavor. Firm flesh. Moderate fat content.	great pompano, permit, golden pompano, Carolina permi, cobblerfish, butterfish, palmenta
Porgy/Scup	Mild flavor. Flaky, but coarse grain. Many bones. Low fat content. Best prepared simply. Large fish have better flavor and fewer bones.	grass porgy, jolthead, Pacific porgy, porgy, scup, white bone

Fish Families	Flavor, Texture, Fat Content and Hints	Species
Salmon	Rich, distinctive flavor. Firm, yet flaky flesh of light pink to red color. The more red the flesh, the richer the taste.	Atlantic salmon, chinook salmon, chum salmon, coho salmon, humpback salmon, keta salmon, king salmon, pink salmon, red salmon, spring salmon, silver salmon, silverside salmon, sockeye salmon
Shark	Distinctive flavor, like swordfish. Very firm, meat-like flesh. Soak in saltwater or milk before cooking to neutralize strong flavor. No bones. Tough cartilage.	blue shark, bull shark, dogfish shark, grayfish shark, greyfish shark, leopard shark, mako shark, pinback shark, tiger shark, thresher shark
Smelt	Rich flavor. Firm, yet tender flesh. Bony best pan fried.	candlelight fish, frostfish, icefish, whitebait

Fish Families	Flavor, Texture, Fat Content and Hints	Species
Sole	Mild, disinctive flavor. Tender, flaky flesh. Very low fat content.	butter sole, curlfin sole, Dover sole, English sole, lemon sole, petrale sole, rex sole, rock sole, sand sole
Sturgeon	Strong flavor, like swordfish and shark. Firm, dry flesh. Low fat content.	green sturgeon, white sturgeon
Swordfish	Strong flavor, like sturgeon and shark. Firm, meatlike flesh. Moderate fat content. When cooking, needs frequent basting.	broadbill

Fish Families	Flavor, Texture, Fat Content and Hints	Species
Tilefish	Mild flavor. Firm, yet tender flesh. Compares to scallops in texture. Low fat content.	blackline tilefish, ocean tilefish, sand tilefish
Trout	Mild, yet distinctive flavor. Firm flesh. Moderate fat content.	brook trout, brown trout, cutthroat trout, Dolly Varden trout, golden trout, lake trout, rainbow trout

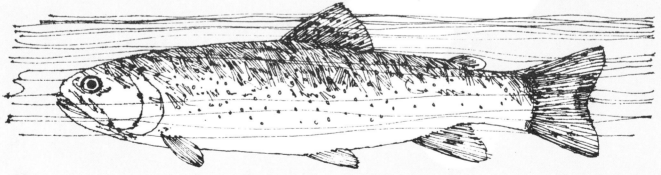

SHELLFISH

Shellfish, the most popular of all seafood, are lean, nutritious and easily digested. Coupled with the fact that they are also high in minerals, they are a boon to dieters and health conscious people alike.

ABALONE

The only place in the United States where abalone are found, are in the coastal waters of California. From the warm tides of Southern Baja, to the cold waters of the California/Oregon border, divers search for these succulent mollusks. They can usually be found clinging to the underside of a large rock.

Although you can only enjoy fresh abalone in California (because abalone faces extinction, and is not allowed to be sold outside of California), frozen abalone from Mexico and Japan are available at most markets.

The edible part of the abalone, the muscle, or "foot," is housed in a 5 to 9-inch oval shell. The inside of the shell is the renown mother-of-pearl.

To prepare the abalone, detach it from the shell. Remove and discard the entrails.

Trim and discard black flesh along rim of abalone. Wash the abalone thoroughly. What you now have is a creamy, white "hat-shaped" object. To make the abalone really tender, place it on a firm, flat surface and whack it quite hard with a large flat board (a 2 x 8-inch piece of lumber is ideal). The preceding step is not essential, but will facilitate the tenderizing, or pounding. Cut the abalone into 1/2-inch slices, vertically. Begin slicing at the crown of the "hat" and end at the brim. Pound each slice with a mallet to about 1/4-inch.

To pan fry: Dip abalone slices into two beaten eggs. Roll slices in 1-1/2 cups flour, seasoned to taste with salt and pepper (preferably white). Chill slices for at least 30 minutes, to allow coating to adhere. Heat 1/4-inch of vegetable oil in a heavy skillet to 375°F. Fry slices about 2 to 3 minutes on each side, or until golden. Do not overcook, or abalone will toughen. Drain slices on paper towels. Serve immediately. One medium-sized abalone should serve about 4 people.

CLAMS AND MUSSELS

Clams are found off both East and West Coasts. Although there is a difference in varieties, most are interchangeable in recipes. Some of the most common clams are the soft-shelled, or long-necked (from Cape Cod and north); hard-shelled (from Cape Cod and south); butter clams; razors; pismos and geoducks. Little necks are the smallest, cherrystone the midsize and guahog the largest.

When you purchase them live, tap their shell. They should close tightly. Discard any that do not.

Whether you buy them, or dig them yourself, all clams need to be scrubbed with a stiff brush before cooking. Also, remove any beard. A little hair-like substance that hangs from clams and mussels.

If you have dug them yourself, they need to be purged. Soak clams in a solution of one gallon of water, one cup of salt and one cup of cornmeal for eight hours. Set them in a cool place to purge.

To shuck clams: Hold a clean clam in your hand with the hinge against the palm. Insert a narrow, sharp knife between the shells. Cut around the edge to release the muscle. Twist and pry to open.

Clams should be eaten the day they are shucked, or frozen after they are shucked for as long as three months. Defrost in the refrigerator, not at room temperature.

CRABS

There are many varieties of crab, and most are interchangeable in recipes. The favorites of the west coast are the Alaskan King crab, which inhabits the waters of the Pacific Northwest (from six to twenty pounds), and the Dungeness crab, found from Alaska to Mexico (one to three pounds). A popular crab of the Atlantic and Gulf Coasts is the Blue crab (which is also the soft-shelled crab while molting). It can weigh from one quarter to one pound while "hard" and from two ounces to one-third pound while "soft." Another common crab in this area is the Rock crab. It is small and averages only one-third of a pound in weight.

Crabs must be alive when they are cooked. The meat must be cooked before it is removed from the shell.

To boil crab: In large kettle, bring about eight quarts of water and two table-spoons of salt to boil. Wash crab thoroughly in cool water. Immerse two or three at a time in boiling water. Boil Blue crabs 8 minutes per pound. Dungenness crab takes only 20 minutes altogether.

To open crab: You may wish to protect your hands by wearing rubber gloves or a potholder glove. Twist and break off all claws and legs.

For Blue crabs, lift up skirt and break it off.

Force upper shell off. It may be necessary to use a knife.

Separate the shell from the body.

Remove and discard spongy material, gills, intestines and sandbags.

Pull meat apart.

Break claws with nutcracker or mallet to loosen meat.

LOBSTERS

This may well be the most popular of all shellfish. There are two varieties of lobster. The ones from New England are the largest and most delicious, and their exceptionally large claws are very meaty. The small Pacific, or rock lobsters are found on the southwest coast of the United States. The meat of this lobster however, is found exclusively in the tail, and their claws contain almost no meat.

Like crab, lobster should be purchased alive.

To boil live lobster: In a large kettle, boil enough water, plus one tablespoon of salt per quart of water, to cover the lobster. Pick up lobster behind large, front claws. Plunge, head first, into boiling water. Cover the kettle. A one pound lobster takes about 7 minutes to cook. 10 minutes should be ample for a two pound lobster. A hint: Small lobsters are the most tender. Remove lobster when done, and submerge in cold water to stop cooking process. Rinse and drain.

To clean and serve boiled lobster: Using a sharp, heavy knife, cut the lobster lengthwise from head to tail. Split it completely in two.

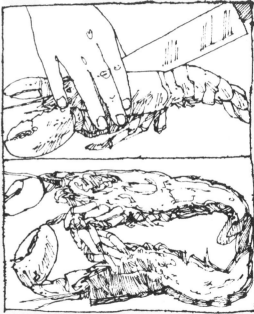

Holding lobster open remove and discard stomach and intestinal vein. The liver and Coral are considered to be delicasies. You may remove them and serve them with the lobster, or throw them away.

As soon as you have cleaned the lobster, serve it. My family likes it best with lots of melted butter and lemon juice. The Coral is delicious mixed with butter. Use about 1/4 to 1/2 cup of soft butter and mash it with the Coral from one lobster. Then spread on lobster meat.

To eat claws, crack them with a nutcracker or smash them with a mallet. Pick out meat with a small fork.

Another fine way to prepare lobster is to broil it.

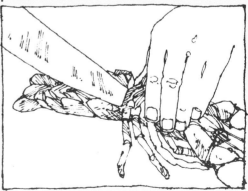

To broil lobster: Hold lobster on its back and sever the tail from the body with a sharp, heavy knife. This snaps the spinal cord and painlessly kills the lobster.

Next, cut the lobster in half lengthwise.

Remove and discard stomach and intestinal vein. Remove Coral and liver and reserve or discard.

Crack the claws.

Preheat broiler pan. Place lobster flesh side up on broiler pan. Brush shell and meat with butter.

Put lobster in oven four inches from the heat source. Broil 10 to 12 minutes, depending upon the size of the lobster, or cook until lightly browned. Serve immediately with more melted butter and lemon juice. Pick out meat from tail and claws with a small fork.

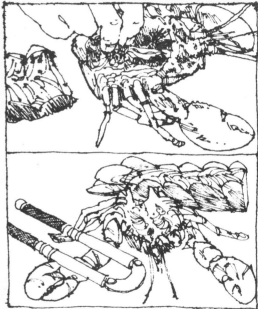

CRAYFISH

A crustacean related to the lobster, but much smaller. It is also known as the crawfish, crawdad, ecrevisse or mudbug. Crayfish can be found almost everywhere. They inhabit quiet streams, ponds, rivers, lakes, creeks and canals. You'll find them moving lazily around a depth of from one to ten feet. You can catch your own by hand, or buy them at your local market.

To prepare a crayfish to cook: Lay it on its back and with a sharp knife, cut it in half lengthwise.

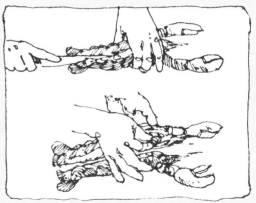

Remove its stomach and intestinal vein. Remove and reserve or discard the Coral and liver.

To boil: Prepare crayfish to cook (see above). Bring enough water to boil to cover crayfish while they cook, plus one tablespoon of salt for each quart of water. Plunge crayfish in head first and boil about 8 minutes, or until they turn bright red. Cover pot tightly while they boil

To bake: Prepare crayfish to cook (see above). Place in preheated 400°F. oven, on a baking dish, for 15 to 20 minutes, or until lightly browned. Baste them frequently, as they have a tendency to dry out.

To eat: Pull tail away from body. Crack claws. Pick out meat from tail and claws with a small fork. If desired, mix Coral with 1/4 to 1/2 cup soft butter and serve with crayfish. Or, serve with plain melted butter and lemon juice.

Because of their small size, eating crayfish is a messy process. So, wear a bib, and dig right in.

SHRIMP AND PRAWNS

These tasty little morsels are popular everywhere. They are available throughout the country in just about every form. Shrimp are sold in sizes ranging from small to jumbo. Prawns can be used in place of shrimp.

Both may be cooked with or without their shells. Purists feel that they retain a better flavor when they are left in their shells.

To shell and devein: Pull off and discard tiny legs. A long slender device, available in the housewares department of most stores, will enable you to shell and devein in one quick stroke. If you don't have one of these, simply peel off skin. You may leave on, or pull off, tail. Remove the sand vein by cutting along the top side of the shrimp with a small knife or your finger.

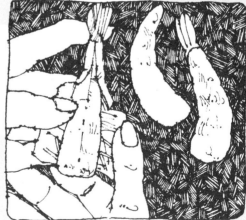

Rinse under cold water.

To butterfly: After deveining, make a deep cut along the back, cutting almost, but not completely, through the body.

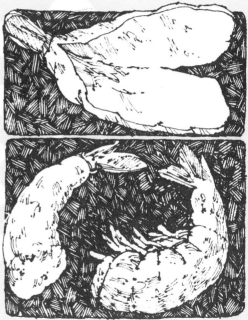

To cook shrimp or prawns: Bring one quart of water and two tablespoons of salt to a boil. Drop in one to two pounds of shelled or unshelled shrimp or prawns. Turn down heat. Simmer for 3 minutes. Be carefull not to overcook. As soon as they turn pink, they are done.

OYSTERS

These fine mollusks are found on both the east and west coasts. They are sold live or shucked. Make sure when you buy them that they close tightly when you tap their shell. Oysters that do not close tightly when tapped are dead and inedible. Some of the more popular varieties include blue point, from the east, and Pacific Coast or Olympia variety. Small oysters have a mild flavor. The large, Pacific Coast oysters have a strong flavor.

To clean and shell: Scrub oysters with a stiff brush and run under cold water. To open oyster, you may wish to "bill" it first. To do this, hammer off a small section of the flat shell, not the round, at the unhinged edge. This will make it easier to shuck.

50

Next, force a thin, yet sturdy, knife between the two shells at the unhinged end of the oyster. It is best to wear gloves as you do this. Twist the knife, until the shells come apart (this may take awhile). Cut the muscle from each shell.

If you are serving the oysters raw, "on the half shell," discard the flat shell. Serve the oyster on the round shell, arranged in a bed of rock salt.

If you prefer oysters slightly cooked, poaching is a good method. Many recipes call for this preparation, rather than for raw oysters.

To poach oysters: Bring two cups of water and one half teaspoon of salt to a boil in a frying pan. Add one cup of shucked oysters. Lower heat, and simmer 4 to 6 minutes. Do not overcook. Oysters are done when their edges begin to curl and they appear "plump."

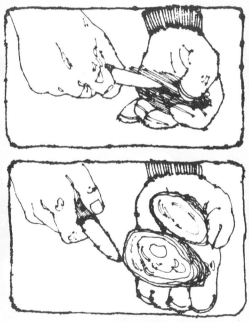

APPETIZERS

Both fish and shellfish make delicious appetizers. No matter what you are planning for the rest of the meal, they offer a refreshing change from crackers and cheese.

You may be tempted to forego appetizers because you believe they are more trouble and expense than they are worth. Because shellfish is costly, I have "stretched" the recipes in which they appear to serve as many people as possible. Most of my recipes utilize inexpensive fish. **Seviche** and **Fiskerfrikadeller** call for any firm, white fish in season. The spectacular results you receive from these recipes belie their low cost and ease of preparation.

CRAB AND CHUTNEY DELUXE

This savory combination could not be easier to prepare.

1 pkg. (8 ozs.) cream cheese
1/4 cup chutney

1 can (5 ozs.) crab meat, drained
crisp unsalted crackers

Place cream cheese on serving plate. Spread chutney over top. Arrange crab on chutney. Serve with crackers. Makes about 18 servings.

SCALLOP WHIRLS

24 scallops, defrosted if frozen
12 strips bacon

wooden toothpicks

Pat scallops dry with paper towel. Cut bacon strips in half. Wrap a half-strip of bacon around each scallop. Secure with a toothpick. Broil 6'' from heat source about 3 to 4 minutes until bacon is crisp and scallop tender. Makes 24 pieces.

OLIVE OYSTER DIP

1 can (6.6 ozs.) smoked oysters
1 pkg. (8 ozs.) cream cheese, softened
1/2 cup minced ripe olives

1 tsp. lemon juice
1/8 tsp. garlic salt

Drain oysters reserving liquid. Chop. Add oyster liquor to cream cheese and blend well. Carefully blend in remaining ingredients, including oysters. Serve with crisp crackers. Makes about 1-1/2 cups.

SHRIMP DIP

2 cans (6 ozs. each) shrimp
3 tbs. catsup
3 tbs. dry sherry

2 tbs. horseradish
1 pkg. (8 ozs.) cream cheese, softened

Rinse the shrimp in cold water and drain well. Mix with remaining ingredients. Chill a few hours to blend flavors. Serve with your favorite thin crackers or vegetables. Makes about 2 cups.

 **ANGELS ON HORSEBACK**

An easy and delicious way to enjoy oysters.

6 thin slices bacon
12 small, fresh, shucked oysters
salt, pepper and paprika to taste
tabasco sauce, if desired
12 wooden toothpicks
4 lemon wedges, if desired
12 small melba toasts, if desired

Fry or broil bacon until limp, but not brown. Cut each strip in half. Sprinkle each oyster with salt, pepper, paprika and 1 drop of tabasco sauce, if desired. Wrap oysters with half strip each of bacon. Secure with toothpick. Broil oysters about 2 minutes on each side, or until bacon is crisp. If desired, top melba toasts with 1 oyster each. Arrange attractively on serving platter with lemon wedges. Makes 12 appetizers.

 # HOT CRAB SPREAD

Keep this spread warm for your guests by placing it in a chafing dish or fondue pot. Surround it with a variety of crackers. A rich and satisfying appetizer that goes well with cocktails.

1 pkg. (8 ozs.) of cream cheese
2 tbs. dijon type, strong flavored mustard
1 can (7-1/2 ozs.) crabmeat
assorted crackers

Melt cream cheese in double boiler over high heat. Add mustard. Stir well. Flake crabmeat. Add to cream cheese mixture. Heat thoroughly. Transfer mixture to chafing dish or fondue pot. Arrange crackers on tray and place next to crab spread. Makes 6 appetizer servings.

 # MARINATED SHRIMP

These shrimp develop an agreeable tart flavor after marinating.

2 lbs. fresh, raw shrimp
2 medium onions, thinly sliced
1-1/2 cups vegetable oil
1-1/2 cups white vinegar
1/2 cup sugar
1-1/2 tsp. **each** salt and celery seed
4 tbs. capers with juice

Peel and devein shrimp (see page 48). Bring one quart of water and two tablespoons of salt to a boil. Simmer shrimp in water for about three minutes, or until they turn pink. Drain. Rinse in cold water to stop cooking process. Chill. When cold, alternate layers of shrimp and onion rings in a sealable container. Mix remaining ingredients. Pour over shrimp. Seal container. Refrigerate for six hours or more. Shake container every hour or so. Remove shrimp from marinade. Arrange attractively on serving platter. Makes about 18 servings.

 **STEAMERS**

For a typical New England style dinner, begin your meal with steamers and serve Maine lobster as your entree.

1 quart soft shelled clams (little necks)
4 cups Court Bouillon (page 133) or water
1/4 cup melted butter

Scrub clams well. In a large Dutch oven type pan, bring Court Bouillon to a boil. Add steamers. Reduce heat. Simmer clams covered about 5 to 7 minutes, or until they are opened. Serve with melted butter. Makes 2 to 4 servings.

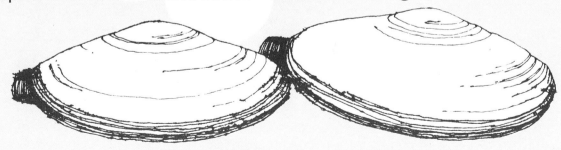

 ## CLAMS CASINO

1 dozen cherrystone clams
rock salt, enough to fill oven proof baking
   in which you cook clams (optional)
3 slices bacon, diced
1/3 cup **each** finely chopped onion and celery
1/4 cup finely chopped green pepper

1 tbs. lemon juice
1 tsp. seasoned salt
1/4 tsp. **each** pepper
   and Worcestershire sauce
1 tbs. catsup
1/4 tsp. seafood seasoning

Scrub clams well. Place in large frying pan with water 1-inch deep. Cover and bring to boil. Simmer about 3 minutes, just until clams begin to open. When clams are cool enough to handle, break off half the shell. With a small knife, pull clam away from shell, but do not remove it from shell. Arrange clams on rock salt in baking dish, or in baking dish without rock salt. Fry bacon a few minutes, until it has rendered some of its fat. Add onion, celery and green pepper. Saute mixture until vegetables are cooked. Add remaining ingredients. Heat. Spoon mixture over clams. Bake at 400°F. for 4 to 5 minutes, just until the edges of the clams begin to curl. Do not over-cook, or the clams will toughen. Makes 4 to 6 servings.

 **MOULES MARINIERE**

This is an adaption of a French recipe. It tastes much like clams Bordelaise.

2 quarts mussels
1/2 cup butter (1 stick)
1/2 cup chopped green onion
3 cloves garlic, minced
pinch of thyme

1 bay leaf
1/4 tsp. white pepper
1 cup dry white wine
2 tbs. chopped parsley
French bread (optional)

Scrub mussels well. Melt butter in Dutch oven type pan or large kettle. Add onions and garlic. Saute 5 minutes. Add thyme, bay leaf, pepper, wine and mussels. Cover tightly. Shake pan a few times to distribute liquid. Simmer about 8 minutes, or until most of the mussels are open. Discard any mussels that are not open. Place mussels in individual soup bowls. Spoon wine mixture over mussels. Sprinkle with parsley. Serve with French bread. Makes 4 servings.

 **FISKERFRIKADELLER**

This is a delicious Danish hors d'oeuvre. It is also good as a light dinner. A food processor will make quick work of this recipe.

1 lb. lean white fish, skinned and deboned
1/4 cup flour
3 tbs. butter, melted
1/2 tsp. salt
pepper to taste
1 egg, well beaten

1 tsp. dill
1/4 cup cream
about 1/4 cup oil
Mustard sauce **or** Hollandaise sauce
  (optional, see pages 163 and 166)

Grind fish in food processor, or in blender. If using blender, grind fish in small amounts. If using food processor all fish may be added at once. Add flour, butter, salt, pepper, egg, and dill to fish. If using blender, remove fish and add ingredients by hand, or by electric mixer. Slowly add cream. Heat oil in skillet to 375°F. Drop fish mixture into oil a tablespoon at a time. Fry until brown on both sides. Drain on paper towels. Serve immediately with Mustard or Hollandaise sauce.

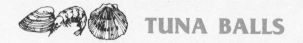 **TUNA BALLS**

These tasty tidbits can be made up to two days ahead of time and kept refrigerated in airtight containers.

2 cans (6-1/2 ozs. each) tuna in oil, drained and flaked
2 cups dried bread crumbs
1/4 cup chopped parsley
1/2 cup finely chopped onion
1 can condensed chicken consomme, undiluted
1 egg, beaten
1/2 cup mayonnaise
1/2 tsp. celery salt
1 tsp. **each** poultry seasoning and dry mustard
1 cup crushed cornflake **or** Triscuit crumbs

Combine all ingredients, except cornflake or Triscuit crumbs. Form into 1-inch balls. Roll in crumbs. Bake at 450°F. for 10 minutes. Makes about 50 balls.

 **SEVICHE**

Raw fish is very popular in Japan and certain South American countries. The fish in this recipe will appear cooked to all but the most trained eye. The lime juice, in which it marinates, actually firms the fish and turns it opaque. Serve in a wide and pretty bowl, next to a small dish of toothpicks for a marvelous appetizer.

1 lb. fresh white fish (red snapper, blackfish, flounder or turbot)
1 cup fresh lime juice
1 ripe tomato, diced
1/4 cup sliced green onion

1 can (4 ozs.) diced green chiles
1/4 tsp. ground oregano
salt and pepper to taste
cilantro or parsley, chopped (optional)

Cut fish into 1/2-inch cubes. Arrange in a single layer in a glass dish. Add remaining ingredients, except cilantro. Stir well. Cover and chill for at least 6 hours, or until fish turns completely white. Serve in marinade, garnished with cilantro. Makes 10 to 12 servings.

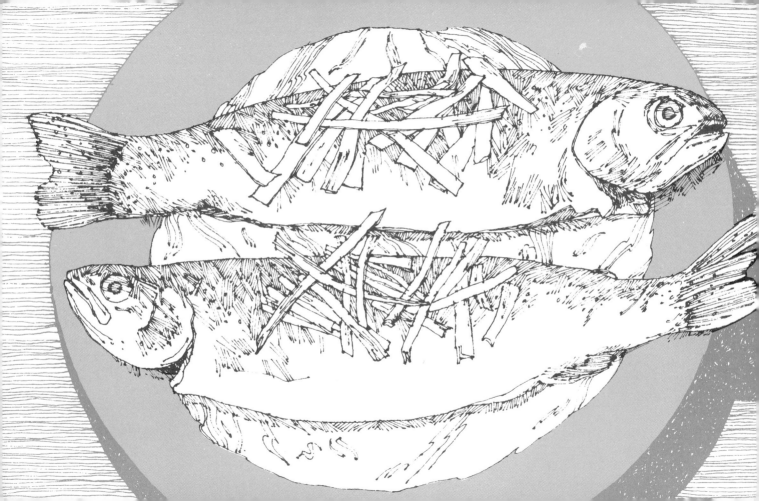

MAIN DISHES

Seafood offers more variety and greater nutrition than beef. Yet, only in the last few years has the general public become aware of its value. The current emphasis on "keeping fit," and health foods, has finally brought seafood into the limelight.

Fish, and especially shellfish, have significantly fewer calories and fat than beef. For example, a three ounce hamburger patty has about 316 calories and 26 grams of fat, while three ounces of salmon, which is considered an "oily," or rich fish, contains about 140 calories and 7.1 grams of fat. An even more striking example is crabmeat. It has about 89 calories and 2.5 grams of fat.

Eating salmon or crab for dinner might allow a weightwatcher to splurge on dessert. Seafood is also recommended for people on low carbohydrate diets.

Whether you're on a special diet, or simply enjoy the adventure of delicious, yet healthy eating, seafood entrees may be just what you need to spark your appetite at dinner time.

TROUT BAKED WITH BACON

This recipe was created by a trout fisherman friend of mine.

Two 3/4 to 1 pound fresh trout, cleaned and split
8 slices bacon
salt and pepper to taste
2 tbs. chopped parsley, if desired
4 lemon wedges, if desired

Rinse and pat dry trout with paper towels. Arrange bacon in a 13 x 9 x 2-inch baking dish. Place trout on top of bacon. Sprinkle with salt and pepper. Cover baking dish with foil. Bake in 375°F. oven for about 20 minutes, or until fish flakes. When done, remove trout to serving platter. Arrange bacon on trout, or discard. Sprinkle with parsley. Serve with lemon wedges. Makes 4 servings.

 ## GOURMET FLATFISH

A classic **duxelle** mixture, which consists of mushrooms, onions and herbs, bakes beneath any fish from the flatfish family. If the boss is coming to dinner, this is guaranteed to please.

1 tbs. salad oil
1 tbs. flour
1/4 cup finely chopped mushrooms
1/3 cup finely chopped onions
3/4 tsp. crushed tarragon leaves
1/4 cup dry white wine, **or** fish stock
1/4 cup cream **or** milk

2 lbs. flatfish fillets (such as turbot, dab, fluke or sole), skins removed
salt, pepper and paprika to taste
1/4 cup dry bread crumbs
2 tbs. melted butter
1 cup shredded, mild cheese

Pour oil into a 13 x 9 x 2-inch baking dish. Stir in flour. Sprinkle mushrooms, onions and tarragon over flour. Stir in wine and cream. Dry fillets with paper towels. Place them over **duxelles** mixture. Combine salt, pepper, paprika and bread crumbs. Sprinkle over fish. Pour melted butter over crumbs. Bake at 350°F. for 20 minutes. Add cheese and bake for 5 minutes longer. Makes 4 to 5 servings.

 **SOLE AMANDINE**

1 lb. fillet of sole

1/4 cup sliced almonds

5 tbs. butter

1/2 tsp. salt

1/4 tsp. pepper

1/2 cup flour

1 cup fish stock, clam juice, **or** chicken broth

1 tbs. lemon juice

1 tbs. chopped parsley

1/2 tsp. tarragon

Pat fillets dry. Saute sliced almonds in 1 tablespoon butter. Watch carefully so they brown, but do not burn. Set aside. Melt 2 tablespoons butter in large skillet. Mix salt and pepper with 1/4 cup plus 2 tablespoons of flour. Roll fillets in flour mixture. Saute fillets in skillet over medium-high heat, about 2 to 3 minutes on each side, or until golden. Remove fish. Arrange attractively on an oven-proof platter. Reduce heat of skillet to medium. Add remaining 2 tablespoons of butter. Scrape the bottom of the skillet as the butter melts. Add remaining 2 tablespoons of flour. Stir until flour is absorbed. Add stock, lemon juice, parsley and tarragon. Bring to a boil. Simmer 2 minutes, until mixture is thickened. Spoon over fish. Sprinkle with almonds. Broil 2 minutes. Makes 4 servings.

# SOLE SURPRISES

1-1/2 to 2 lbs. sole fillets (8 pieces)
1/4 lb. small shrimp, cooked, shelled
    and deveined (see page 48)
1/4 cup fine dry bread crumbs
1/2 tsp. fine herbes
1/4 tsp. onion salt

1/4 tsp. dill
1/4 cup grated Parmesan cheese
3 tbs. mayonnaise
1 can cream of shrimp soup, undiluted
2 tbs. dry sherry
chopped chives, for garnish (optional)

Dry fish with paper towels. Grease 4, six-ounce Pyrex custard cups. Arrange two pieces of fish in an "X" pattern in the cups. Make sure to have the fillets touching the sides and bottom of the cups. Fillets will overlap and hang out the sides of the cups quite a bit. Stir together shrimp, bread crumbs, fines herbes, onion salt, dill, Parmesan cheese and mayonnaise. Divide mixture among fillets and stuff. Fold excess fish over filling, completely enclosing the filling. Bake at 350°F. for 30 to 40 minutes. Just before fish is done, heat soup and sherry together in a saucepan. When fish is done, turn cups upside down on a serving platter. Spoon sauce over fillets. If desired, sprinkle with chives. Makes 4 servings.

TURBOT PARMESAN

Turbot is a delicate flatfish which can be used in any flounder or sole recipe.

1-1/2 lbs. turbot fillets (or any flatfish)
1/2 tsp. salt
pepper to taste
3/4 cup sour cream
1/2 cup grated Parmesan cheese
1 tbs. chives
1/4 cup fine dry bread crumbs
paprika
watercress (optional)

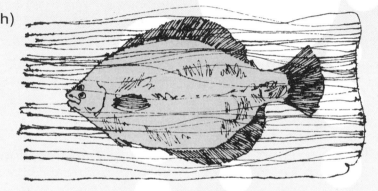

Wash and pat turbot dry with paper towels. Arrange in greased baking pan. Sprinkle salt and pepper over fish. Mix sour cream with cheese, chives and crumbs. Spread over fish. Dust with paprika. Bake at 450°F. for 10 minutes, just until fish flakes. Garnish with watercress. Makes 4 servings.

# BAKED TILEFISH WITH TOMATO SAUCE

Tile is a marvelous fish that is caught in very deep, mid-Atlantic waters. If this is not available in your area, choose any firm, mild flavored fish such as flounder or sole.

1-1/2 lbs. fish fillets
1 can (8 ozs.) tomato sauce
1/2 cup finely chopped onion
1/2 tsp. Bon Appetit seasoning (Schilling)
1 tbs. oil
2 tbs. fresh lemon juice

Grease a baking dish. Arrange fillets in a single layer. Mix remaining ingredients. Pour over fish. Bake at 400°F. for 10 to 12 minutes, or until fish flakes. Makes 4 servings.

SHRIMP STUFFED TILEFISH

If you cannot find tilefish, you may substitute any member of the flatfish family (see chart, beginning on page 25).

1-1/2 lbs. tilefish, butterfly cut (see page 5), **or** thick fillets
1/4 lb. fresh shrimp, shelled and deveined, **or** 1 can (6 ozs.) shrimp, drained
1/2 cup grated Havarti, Gruyére, **or** Swiss cheese
1/4 cup sliced green onions, including tops
1/2 tsp. salt
1/2 tsp. dill
2 tbs. mayonnaise
wooden toothpicks
2 tbs. butter, melted
3 tbs. lemon juice
1 lemon, sliced (optional)
parsley sprigs (optional)

If you cannot find butterfly cut, slice the thick fillets almost all the way through.

74

Arrange fish in a greased, glass baking dish. Mix the shrimp, cheese, onions, salt, dill and mayonnaise together. Divide mixture among fillets and stuff. Secure closed with wooden toothpicks, only if needed. Mix butter and lemon juice together. Pour over fillets. Bake at 350ºF. for about 30 minutes. If desired, garnish with lemon slices and parsley. Makes 4 servings.

CRAB STUFFED FILLETS

No last minute preparation with this elegant recipe. The sauce bakes right along with the fillets

2 lbs. firm, white fish fillets	freshly ground pepper
1 lb. crabmeat	1/4 tsp. dry mustard or curry
wooden toothpicks	1/2 cup grated Parmesan cheese
1 can cream of shrimp soup, undiluted	paprika

Dry fillets with paper towel. Divide crabmeat between fillets. Spread fillets with crabmeat. Roll fillets, beginning from one tapered end and rolling toward the other. Secure with wooden toothpicks. Place in buttered baking dish. Mix together soup, pepper and mustard. Spoon over fish. Sprinkle with cheese and paprika. Bake at 350°F. for about 25 minutes. Remove toothpicks. Arrange on platter and spoon sauce over fillets. Serve immediately. Makes 8 servings.

 **HERB BROILED FISH**

Any fish fillets or steaks may be used, but scrod, a young cod, is especially good

1-1/2 lbs. fish fillet (any fish from cod or flatfish families,
  see chart beginning on page 25).
1/4 cup butter
1/8 tsp. salt
1/8 tsp. pepper
1/2 tsp. seafood seasoning
1/4 tsp. tarragon
1/2 tsp. dry mustard

Preheat broiler. Arrange fish on greased baking pan. Melt butter and add remaining ingredients. Pour half over fish. Broil 5 minutes. Turn. Baste with remaining herb/butter mixture. Broil about 5 minutes longer, or until fish flakes. Makes 4 servings.

 # GOLDEN FILLETS

Children love fish prepared this way.

1-1/2 to 2 lbs. fillets (any firm, mild flavored
    fish such as haddock, flounder or sole)
1/4 cup butter
1/2 cup dried bread crumbs
1/4 cup Parmesan cheese

1/2 tsp. garlic salt
1/4 tsp. fines herbes
1/2 cup mayonnaise
fresh parsley (optional)
lemon wedges (optional)

Rinse and pat fish dry with paper towels. Cut into 4 or 5 pieces. Add butter to a shallow baking dish. Place in 350°F. oven to melt. Mix crumbs, cheese, salt and herbs. Spread mayonnaise on one side of the fish. Roll mayonnaise side in crumb mixture. Repeat on other side of fish. Remove baking dish from oven and arrange fish in a single layer. Turn over to coat with melted butter. Sprinkle leftover crumbs on top. Measure height of fish at highest point. Bake at 425°F. for 10 minutes for each inch of height (i.e., a one-inch fish takes 10 minutes). Garnish with chopped parsley. Serve with lemon wedges. Makes 4 to 5 servings.

 **SPICY COD BAKE**

Cod is popular and abundant fish throughout the world.

1 lb. cod fillets
1/2 lb. mushrooms
2 carrots
1 medium-sized onion
salt and pepper

juice of 1/2 lemon
1 cup V-8 or tomato juice
1/4 tsp. dry mustard
1 tsp. vinegar
1 tsp. Worcestershire sauce

Rinse and pat dry cod with paper towels. Chop mushrooms, carrots and onion finely. To make this job easy, use a food processor. Spread half of this mixture in a greased baking dish. Arrange fillets in a single layer on top. Sprinkle with salt and pepper. Squeeze lemon juice over the fish. Spread remaining vegetable mixture on top of fish. Mix V-8, mustard, vinegar and Worcestershire sauce. Pour over the fish. Bake at 400°F. for 20 minutes. Makes 4 servings.

 ## BAKED FISH IN WHITE WINE

3 to 3-1/2 lbs. any firm white fish
1/2 medium onion, sliced
3 shallots, minced
1 cup sliced mushrooms
1 tbs. lemon juice
salt and pepper to taste
pinch **each** nutmeg and cloves

dry white wine
2 tbs. brandy
2 tbs. flour
2 tbs. soft butter
dash cayenne
parsley (optional)
lemon slices (optional)

Dry fish with paper towels. Butter a large baking dish and arrange fish in it. Separate onions into rings. Scatter over fish. Combine shallots, mushrooms, lemon juice, salt, pepper, nutmeg and cloves. Sprinkle over fish and onions. Almost cover the fish with wine. Bake at 350°F. for 20 to 30 minutes, or until fish flakes. Remove from oven. With a baster, remove all cooking liquid to a small saucepan. Reduce liquid over high heat to 1-1/4 cups. Warm brandy in a ladle. Light it carefully. Pour flaming brandy into reduced liquid. Set aside. Cream together flour and butter. Add to liquid. Stir mixture constantly over medium heat. When thick, add cayenne and pour over fish. Garnish with parsley and lemons. Makes 8 servings.

# BAKED HAKE TARRAGON

Hake is similar to cod, and may be substituted in any recipe calling for cod. It is almost fat free, tasty and sweet.

1-1/2 lbs. hake fillets (or cod, haddock, burbot, ling, pollock, scrod)
salt and pepper to taste
3 tbs. butter, melted
1/2 tsp. fresh tarragon, **or** 1/4 tsp. dried tarragon, crushed
1/4 tsp. Bon Appetit seasoning (Schilling)
paprika
parsley (optional)
lemon wedges (optional)

Dry fillets with paper towel. Place in single layer in a shallow, greased baking dish. Sprinkle with salt and pepper. Combine butter, tarragon and Bon Appetit. Pour over fish. Sprinkle with paprika. Bake at 400°F. about 15 minutes, until fish flakes. Garnish with parsley and lemon wedges. Makes 4 servings.

 # NORTHWOODS MUSKIE

The largest of the pike family, the muskellunge is found in fresh water lakes throughout the area of the Great Lakes, and sometimes in the Pacific Ocean near Alaska. This easy recipe is the favorite of a champion muskie catcher.

4 to 6 fillets of muskellunge (or any member of the pike family,
    see chart beginning on page 25).
salt and pepper to taste
1/4 cup butter, melted
light cream, enough to cover fish

Arrange fillets in a single layer in a greased baking dish. Salt and pepper to taste. Pour melted butter and cream over fish. Bake at 325°F. for 45 minutes, or until fish flakes. Makes 4 to 6 servings.

POLLOCK EN PAPILLOTTE (in paper)

Pollock is a member of the cod family. If you cannot find it, you may substitute any other lean fish, such as sea bass, hake, pike or red snapper. Very thick fillets are best.

2 lbs. pollock fillets
juice of 1 lemon
1/4 cup butter
1/2 lb. mushrooms, chopped
1/2 cup chopped green onion

salt and pepper to taste
1/2 tsp. dry mustard
1/2 cup mayonnaise
baking parchment

Dry fillets well. If thick, cut almost through, horizontally, with knife.

Squeeze lemon over insides. Melt butter in skillet. Saute mushrooms and green onions. Add salt and pepper. Divide mushroom filling among fillets. If thin, place filling between two fillets. Stuff thick fillets. Mix together mustard and mayonnaise.

Cut 4 large hearts from the baking parchment, about 12 inches wide and 12 inches long.

Place fillet just to the left of center on the heart. Spread fillet with mayonnaise. Bring together edges of heart and roll them tightly shut, to encase fish.

Carefully place hearts on cookie sheet. Bake at 400°F. for 20 minutes, or until papillotte is puffed and brown. Makes 4 servings.

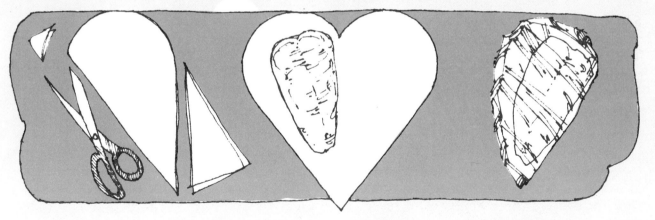

BLACKFISH WITH SPINACH MUSHROOM STUFFING

Absolutely terrific! That's what my family said the first time they tasted this recipe. Although the blackfish is generally a sport fish, it is sometimes found in East Coast markets. Cape Cod to the Delaware Bay is the normal habitat of the blackfish, which is also known as the "tautog."

one, 4 to 5 pound blackfish (or any member of the flatfish family), pan dressed
salt and pepper
1/2 pkg. frozen chopped spinach, defrosted and drained
1/2 cup fresh, sliced mushrooms
wooden toothpicks
1/4 cup butter, melted
2 tbs. lemon juice

Line a shallow baking dish, with foil. Grease foil. Cut off head and tail, if you have not already done so. Rinse and pat dry. Sprinkle cavity with salt and pepper. Put spinach in cavity and spread with mushrooms. Secure fish closed with toothpicks. Mix together butter and lemon juice. Pour over fish. Using a ruler, measure tallest

part of fish. Cook fish 10 minutes per inch. Bake at 400°F. Baste with pan juices when half cooking time is over. This fish does not separate into the "flakes" that most of the others do. Makes 4 to 5 servings.

 ## BROILED MAHI MAHI

Only rarely is Mahi-Mahi available anywhere except on the West Coast and in Hawaii. Substitute with any other fish steaks.

1-1/2 lbs. mahi-mahi steaks
1/2 cup butter **or** margarine
1 clove garlic, minced
1 tsp. soy sauce
2 tbs. lemon juice
1 tbs. minced parsley (optional)

Pat steaks dry with paper towels. Place in greased baking dish in single layer. Melt all but one tablespoon butter. Add garlic and saute until limp. Remove from heat. Stir in soy sauce and lemon juice. Pour over steaks and allow to marinate at least 15 minutes, longer if desired. Broil four inches from heat, turning once, until fish just begins to flake. Cooking time will be about 5 minutes on each side, depending upon thickness of steaks. Garnish with parsley. Makes 4 servings.

# STURGEON WITH WILD RICE

Found in the northwest, southeast, and fresh waters throughout the country, sturgeon is a firm, delicately flavored fish.

1-1/2 lb. sturgeon fillets (swordfish or shark may be substituted)
1/4 cup olive oil
1 small green pepper, seeded and diced
1 medium onion, diced
1/2 tsp. sweet basil
1/2 cup dry white wine
1 can cream of mushroom soup, undiluted
1 cup wild or brown rice, cooked

Cut sturgeon into one-inch squares. Heat oil in skillet. Add green pepper and onions, cooking until tender. Add sturgeon and basil. Fry quickly about 2 minutes on each side. Add wine and soup. Simmer 7 to 10 minutes, or until fish is cooked. Serve over warm rice. Makes 4 servings.

GRILLED SWORDFISH STEAK

The mayonnaise "melts" into the swordfish after cooking, but you'll notice the succulence it lends to the fish.

1 swordfish steak per person (each 3/4 to 1-inch thick)
mayonnaise
lemon butter: For 4 servings, 1/4 cup melted butter and juice of 1 lemon
chopped parsley (optional)

If cooking outside, on a grill, start fire and allow to burn for 20 to 30 minutes. The coals must be very hot. If cooking indoors, preheat broiler. Spread a generous portion of mayonnaise on one side of each steak. If cooking outside, place mayonnaise side down, on grill. If cooking inside, place mayonnaise side up, closest to heating element. Cook about 6 minutes. Turn and spread mayonnaise on other side. Cook for an additional 5 to 8 minutes. Test for doneness by prodding with fork. If it flakes, it is done. Prepare lemon butter. Arrange steaks attractively on serving platter. Garnish with parsley. Serve with lemon butter.

# BROILED SALMON

An easy dish for company when served with Quick Hollandaise Sauce, page 166.

1 salmon steak per serving
1 tsp. butter per serving
1/4 tsp. seafood seasoning per serving
1 tsp. lemon juice per serving
parsley (optional)
Quick Hollandaise Sauce, page 166 (optional)

Preheat broiler. Cover a shallow pan with foil. Arrange salmon on foil. Melt butter. Add seafood seasoning and lemon juice. Pour half over the salmon. Broil three inches from heat for 4 minutes. Turn. Pour remaining butter on salmon. Broil another 4 minutes until salmon flakes. Garnish with fresh parsley and serve with sauce.

MARINATED SALMON

This recipe can also be used for blue fish, Spanish mackerel or swordfish.

1 whole salmon, 5 to 6 lbs.
2/3 cup vinegar
1/3 cup olive oil
1 medium onion, minced
1/4 cup parsley, chopped
2 cloves garlic, minced or mashed
parsley sprigs (optional)

Clean and scale salmon. Remove head and tail, if desired. Serrate flesh by making 1/2-inch slashes in it. Mix vinegar, oil, onion, parsley and garlic. Place salmon in shallow, glass dish. Pour marinade mixture over salmon. Marinate salmon for at least an hour. Broil four inches from heat for 4 minutes. Turn over. Broil 4 minutes longer, until fish is firm and begins to flake. Garnish with parsley sprigs. Serve immediately or chill and serve cold. Makes 8 servings.

SALMON LOAF

If you keep a can of salmon on your pantry shelf, this recipe can be put together quickly at the end of a busy day. Want a change? Try canned tuna or mackeral.

1 can (15 ozs.) salmon
1 cup soft bread crumbs
1/4 cup milk
2 tbs. chopped parsley
1 tbs. lemon juice
1 egg, beaten
Cucumber Sauce, page 165

Drain salmon well. Flake, removing any pieces of skin and bones. Combine bread crumbs and milk. Add fish and remaining ingredients, except sauce. Pat into a greased 9 x 5 x 3-inch pan. Bake at 350°F. for 30 minutes. Serve with Cucumber Sauce. Makes 3 to 4 servings.

SEABURGERS

Use any canned or leftover fish for these delectable sandwiches.

1 can (15-1/2 ozs.) salmon
12 single soda crackers, crumbled
1 egg, beaten
2 tbs. chopped onion
1/4 tsp. pepper
1/2 tsp. celery salt
2 tbs. oil
4 buns
Cucumber Sauce, page 165 (optional)

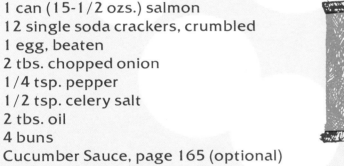

Drain, flake and debone salmon. Mix well with crackers, egg, onion, pepper and celery salt. Shape into 4 patties. Heat oil in skillet. Brown patties quickly on both sides. Place on buns and top with Cucumber Sauce. Makes 4 servings.

STUFFED TOMATOES AU GRATIN

When your garden blesses you with an abundance of giant tomatoes, try this recipe. Any leftover canned or smoked fish may be used.

6 large, ripe tomatoes
salt
2 cups cooked fish, flaked
1 cup cooked rice
3/4 cup grated Swiss cheese
1 egg, beaten
1/2 tsp. oregano
1 tbs. butter, melted
1/4 cup dried bread crumbs

Remove cores and hollow out tomatoes. Sprinkle with salt. Turn over on paper towels. Drain for 15 minutes. Mix fish with rice, cheese, egg and oregano. Fill tomatoes with mixture. Place in greased baking dish. Mix together butter and crumbs. Sprinkle over tomatoes. Bake at 350°F. for 15 minutes. Makes 6 servings.

 **FISH CAKES**

A food processor makes quick work of the chopping. You will want to cook extra fish to have leftovers for this delicious recipe.

1 lb. (2 cups) cooked fish
1 medium onion, finely chopped
1/4 lb. (1-1/2 cups) mushrooms, chopped
2 cups bread crumbs
1 tsp. seasoned salt
1/4 cup chopped parsley

2 eggs, beaten
3 tbs. butter
2 tbs. oil
lemon wedges (optional)
Tartar Sauce

Remove bones from fish. Chop in food processor, or flake by hand very well. Remove to mixing bowl. Add chopped onion and mushrooms. Stir in 1 cup bread crumbs, salt, parsley, and eggs. Form into patties, adding more bread crumbs only if necessary to bind. Coat patties with remaining bread crumbs. Heat butter and oil to bubbling in skillet. Fry patties quickly on each side. Remove to heated platter and place in oven if you cannot fry all patties at once. If desired, serve with lemon wedges and Tartar Sauce. Makes 8 servings.

OPEN FACED FISH SANDWICH

Serve this good tasting favorite with a vegetable soup or fruit salad for a complete meal.

2 cups leftover fish, or 2 cans, 6-1/2 ozs. each, tuna
1/4 cup finely chopped celery (optional)
2 tbs. tartar sauce
1/2 tsp. dillweed
salt and pepper to taste
2 large tomatoes
8 slices bread, toasted
1 cup grated mild cheese

Skin, flake and debone fish. Add celery, if desired. Blend in enough tartar sauce to bind mixture together. Season with dill, salt and pepper. Thinly slice the tomatoes and dry each side on paper towels. Arrange on toast. Spread with fish mixture. Sprinkle cheese on top. Broil four inches from heat source about 3 minutes, until cheese bubbles. Makes 4 servings.

TUNA ELEGANTE

Your family won't groan when you tell them you're serving this tuna casserole for dinner.

2 cans (6-1/2 ozs. each) tuna, drained
1 pkg. (10 ozs.) frozen asparagus, defrosted
   or 1 bunch fresh asparagus
1 can mushroom soup, undiluted
3 cups cooked rice
1 pint cottage cheese

2 tbs. grated onion
1/2 cup sour cream
1/4 cup sliced black olives
2 tbs. butter, melted
1/2 cup bread crumbs

Drain and flake tuna. Reserve six asparagus spears. Cut remainder into 1/4-inch pieces. Mix tuna, asparagus, soup, rice, cottage cheese, onion, sour cream and olives. Pour into greased two quart casserole. Add bread crumbs to melted butter and sprinkle over top. Bake at 350°F. for 30 to 35 minutes. During last 10 minutes of baking time, steam asparagus spears. When casserole is done, garnish with asparagus. Makes 6 servings.

WISCONSIN FISH BOIL

The early Scandanavian settlers of Door County, Penninsula, the "thumb" of Wisconsin, are credited with originating this delightful feast. Now civic clubs and restaurants throughout the area are known for their famous fish boils. In your home you cannot duplicate the final ceremony—pouring kerosene on the outdoor fire to cause a surge of flame and a boiling over of foam and fish oils—but you can duplicate the irresistible flavors of this popular event. The meal is traditionally completed with a tangy coleslaw, several varieties of bread, including light rye, and, finally, cherry pie.

6 fresh or frozen fish steaks cut 1-inch thick
18 small red potatoes in jackets
12 small boiling onions
1 cup salt (yes, this is the correct amount)
1/2 cup butter, melted
2 tbs. chopped parsley (optional)
6 lemon wedges (optional)

Thaw fish if frozen. Fill an 8-quart kettle, which has a basket (similar to a deep fry basket), about 2/3 full of water and heat to a rapid boil. Wash potatoes and remove any deep eyes. Skin onions. When water is boiling rapidly, add salt. The cooked food will not taste too salty. Put potatoes and onions in basket. Boil hard for 18 minutes. Carefully add steaks. Continue to boil rapidly for 12 more minutes. Test with a long fork to be sure the fish and potatoes are cooked. Remove from water and drain. Divide fish, potatoes and onions among six heated plates. Pour melted butter over all. Sprinkle with parsley. Serve with lemon wedges. Makes 6 servings.

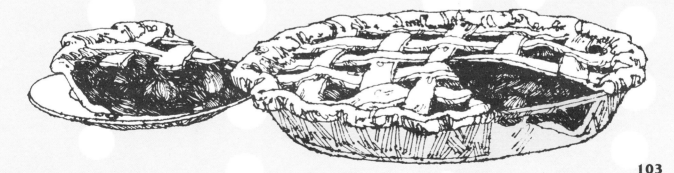

CRAB OR SHRIMP QUICHE

Cheddar cheese adds a hearty flavor to this quiche. For a lighter flavor, add Swiss cheese instead. Cut into slim wedges for a great appetizer.

1 cup crab meat **or** tiny shrimp,
   fresh or canned
4 slices bacon
1 tbs. butter
1 cup sliced, fresh mushrooms
1/4 cup chopped green onion

2 ozs. cream cheese
1 cup light cream or milk
3 eggs, well beaten
1 cup grated Cheddar or Swiss cheese
one 9-inch pastry shell, baked and cooled

Remove any cartilage from crabmeat and discard. Fry bacon until crisp. Drain well. Crumble into small pieces. Melt butter. Add mushrooms and onion. Saute until limp. Add cream cheese. Stir until melted. Beat eggs and cream together. Slowly add to cream cheese mixture. Add crab meat. Heat until mixture is warm. Do not boil, or eggs and cream might curdle. Sprinkle bacon and grated cheese on bottom of pie shell. Gently, pour liquid into shell. Set on baking sheet. Bake at 375°F. for 30 minutes, or until knife inserted into center comes out clean. Makes 4 to 6 servings.

CRAB OR SHRIMP "SOUFFLE"

2 cups fresh, flaked crabmeat, **or**
   2 cups small, fresh shrimp, shelled
   and deveined (see page 48)
1 cup mayonnaise
1/2 cup **each** finely chopped celery
  and onion
1 medium green pepper, chopped
2 tbs. minced parsley

1 tsp. **each** grated lemon peel and salt
1/4 tsp. pepper
8 to 10 slices bread
4 eggs
3 cups milk
1 can mushroom soup, undiluted
1 cup fresh, cooked mushrooms, sliced
1/4 cup grated Parmesan cheese

In a large bowl, combine the crab, mayonnaise, onion, celery, green pepper, parsley, lemon peel, salt and pepper. Cut four slices bread into 1-inch cubes. Place in bottom of greased 3-quart rectangular casserole. Spoon crab mixture over bread cubes. Remove crusts from remaining bread. Fit slices to completely cover crab mixture. Beat eggs slightly. Add milk. Pour over bread. Cover and refrigerate overnight. Bake, uncovered, at 325°F. for about 1 hour. During last 15 minutes, heat soup and mushrooms. Spoon over baked souffle. Sprinkle with Parmesan cheese. Place under broiler 2 minutes to melt cheese. Makes 12 servings.

# SPINACH-CRAB COTTAGE BAKE

Have some leftover fish? Substitute one cup of flaked, cooked fish for the crabmeat in this recipe.

1 can (7 ozs.) crabmeat
1 pkg. (10 ozs.) frozen spinach, defrosted and well drained
1/4 tsp. nutmeg
1 cup cottage cheese
1/3 cup finely chopped onion
1/2 cup grated cheese (such as Provolone, Monterey Jack, Muenster)
1/2 cup tomato juice
1 tsp. Worcestershire sauce
1 tbs. lemon juice

Drain and pick over crab. Combine spinach and nutmeg. Spread in a small, greased casserole. Combine cottage cheese, onion and cheese. Spoon over spinach. Top with crabmeat. Combine remaining ingredients. Pour over crab. Bake at 350°F. for 20 minutes. Makes 4 servings.

MARYLAND CRAB CAKES

Maryland, home of the delicious Blue Crab, offers us these delicacies.

1 lb. crabmeat
1 cup Italian seasoned breadcrumbs
1 egg, beaten
1/4 cup mayonnaise
1/2 tsp. salt
1/4 tsp. pepper
1 tsp. Worcestershire sauce
1 tsp. dry mustard
margarine, butter **or** oil

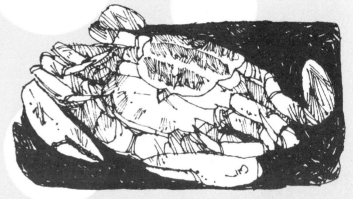

Remove cartilage from crabmeat. Mix breadcrumbs, egg, mayonnaise and seasonings, except margarine. Add crab. Mix gently but thoroughly. Shape into 6 cakes. Fry in skillet on medium-high heat, in just enough fat to prevent sticking. Cook until browned, about 5 minutes per side. Makes 6 cakes.

SCAMPI ALLA ROMANA

Use the largest available shrimp and serve with crusty bread to soak up the marvelous garlic butter.

20 to 24 jumbo or super jumbo shrimp
3/4 cup butter
2 cloves garlic, minced
4 shallots, **or** 1/2 cup green onion, thinly sliced
1 tbs. lemon juice

1 tbs. Worchestershire sauce
dash cayenne pepper
1 tbs. fresh chopped parsley
1/4 cup dry white wine

Peel and devein shrimp, leaving tail attached (see page 48). Melt butter. Add garlic and onions. Stir in lemon juice, Worcestershire sauce, cayenne, parsley and wine. Place shrimp on a heat-proof platter or broiler pan. Pour 1/2 of the garlic butter mixture over the shrimp. Broil five inches from heat for 3 minutes. Turn shrimp over, pour remaining garlic butter mixture over, and broil 3 minutes longer. Allow shrimp to marinate 2 minutes before serving. Makes 4 servings.

SHRIMP MORNAY

You may prepare this ahead of time and simply pop it under the broiler for a few minutes when you are ready to serve it.

1 lb. raw shrimp, cooked, shelled and deveined (see page 48)
    or 1/2 lb. frozen large shrimp, defrosted;
    or 2 cans (4-1/2 ozs. each) canned shrimp, rinsed and drained
2 tbs. butter
2 tbs. flour
1/3 cup cream
1 cup chicken broth
1/4 cup shredded Swiss cheese
1/4 cup grated Parmesan cheese

Prepare shrimp. Melt butter over medium-high heat. Add flour. When bubbly, stir in cream. Add broth. Slowly stir in Swiss cheese. When thick, add shrimp. Divide into four ramekins or baking shells. Top with Parmesan cheese. Broil four inches from heat until bubbly hot and lightly browned. Makes 4 servings.

FRIED SHRIMP

Everyone's favorite. These are even good served cold.

1 lb. jumbo shrimp
peanut oil
Mustard Sauce, page 163

Beer Batter:
1 cup flour
1 tsp. baking powder
1/4 tsp. salt
dash white pepper
1 egg, beaten
1 cup stale beer

Shell and devein shrimp, (see page 48) leave tail on. Pour 1-inch of oil in frying pan. Heat to 375°F. Dip shrimp into batter. Place carefully in oil. Fry about 3 minutes on each side. Serve with Mustard Sauce. Makes 4 servings.

SHRIMPLY DELICIOUS

This dish is also known as Shrimp Harpin. Assemble it the day before you plan to serve it. For a nice touch, spoon it into individual scallop shells and bake it for ten minutes.

2 lbs. large, fresh shrimp, shelled
    and deveined (see page 48)
1 tbs. lemon juice
3 tbs. salad oil
3/4 cup rice, cooked
2 tbs. butter
1/4 cup minced green pepper
1/4 cup finely chopped onion
1 tsp. salt

1/4 tsp. white pepper
1/4 tsp. mace
dash cayenne pepper
1 can (10-1/2 ozs.) tomato soup, undiluted
1 cup heavy cream
1/2 cup dry sherry
1/2 cup slivered almonds
paprika

Place shrimp in large greased casserole. Drizzle lemon juice and oil over shrimp. Gently toss rice with shrimp. In separate pan, melt butter. Add green pepper and onion. Saute 5 minutes. Add salt, white pepper, mace, cayenne, tomato soup, cream

and sherry to sauted mixture. Gently stir into shrimp and rice. Cover mixture and refrigerate overnight. Before baking, top with almonds and sprinkle with paprika. Bake at 350°F. for about 25 minutes. Makes 8 servings.

CHINESE SHRIMP AND CHICKEN

If you have any leftover chicken, try this low calorie dish.

2 tbs. butter
1-1/2 cups diagonally sliced celery
1/4 cup finely chopped onion
1 lb. fresh, raw shrimp, peeled
   and deveined (see page 48)
1 cup sliced, fresh mushrooms

2 cups diced, cooked chicken
1 tbs. cornstarch
2 tbs. soy sauce
1 cup chicken broth
2 cups bean sprouts, **or**
   2 cups fresh chopped spinach

Melt butter in skillet over medium heat. Add celery and onion. Cook 2 minutes. Add shrimp and mushrooms. Cover and cook 2 minutes. Add chicken. Remove pan from heat. Mix together cornstarch, soy sauce and broth. Return pan to heat. Add sauce and cook over medium-high heat until thickened and clear. Add sprouts. Cook 1 minutes. Serve immediately. Makes 6 servings.

SHRIMP AND ARTICHOKE CASSEROLE

1 lb. fresh shrimp, shelled and
   deveined (see page 48) **or** 3/4 lb. frozen
   medium shrimp, defrosted
6 tbs. butter
2 tbs. cornstarch
2 cups milk
1 tsp. salt
1/4 tsp. pepper
1 tbs. Worcestershire sauce

dash Tabasco
1/4 cup dry sherry
1 can (14 ozs.) artichoke hearts
   or 1 pkg. frozen, cooked
1/2 lb. fresh mushrooms, sliced
1/4 cup grated Parmesan cheese
paprika
rice to serve 6

Prepare shrimp. Melt 4 tablespoons butter in saucepan. Blend in cornstarch. Add milk. Boil one minute. Add salt, pepper, Worcestershire sauce, Tabasco and sherry. Drain artichokes, cut in half. Arrange in shallow, greased casserole. Scatter shrimp over artichokes. Melt remaining butter, add mushrooms and saute. Add to the shrimp. Pour white sauce over all. Sprinkle with cheese and paprika. Bake at 350°F. for 20 to 30 minutes. Serve over rice. Makes 6 servings.

SCALLOPED OYSTERS

A perfect dish for brunch, lunch, late dinner or a buffet. Easterners have been preparing oysters this way for generations.

1 qt. shucked oysters (see page 50) in their liquor
4 tbs. cream
1 tsp. Worcestershire sauce
1 cup soft, white bread crumbs
2 cups cracker crumbs
1 cup melted butter

Combine 3/4-cup oyster liquor with cream. If you don't have enough oyster liquor to equal 3/4-cup, add more cream. Stir in Worcestershire sauce. Mix bread and cracker crumbs together. Add butter. Place a thin layer of crumbs on the bottom of a 1-1/2-quart casserole. Add a layer of oysters, 1/3 remaining crumbs and half the oyster liquor-cream mixture. Repeat, ending with crumbs. Don't use more than 2 layers of oysters. Bake at 400°F. for 30 minutes. Makes 6 to 8 servings.

OYSTER LOAVES

Fried oyster sandwiches are as popular in the south as Hoagies, Poor Boys, and Submarines are in the north. In fact, some small shops sell them exclusively.

2 dozen oysters, shucked and
    well drained (see page 50)
1 cup yellow cornmeal **or**
    finely ground bread crumbs
1 tsp. salt
1/4 tsp. pepper

1/8 tsp. cayenne
salad oil
1/4 cup melted butter (optional)
4 rolls or sandwich buns
Garnishes: pickle slices, hot sauce, catsup or
      cocktail sauce (optional)

Rinse oysters and pat dry. Combine cornmeal, salt, pepper and cayenne. Roll each oyster in crumb mixture to coat evenly. Heat one inch of oil to 375°F. Fry oysters about 1 minute on each side, or until golden brown. Drain on absorbent paper. Slice rolls lengthwise. Arrange oysters on bottom half of each roll. Garnish as desired. Top with upper half. Serve immediately. Makes 4 servings.

HANGTOWN FRY

Legend has it that a goldminer who just "struck it rich," road into town one day, struted into the restaurant and shouted "Gimme the most expensive thing on your menu!" An imaginative cook came up with this clever recipe utilizing two of the most rare and expensive ingredients in his mountainous, western town—eggs and oysters.

12 to 18 oysters, shucked if fresh, (see page 50),
    drained if bottled
salt and pepper to taste
3/4 cup finely ground cracker crumbs

7 eggs
4 tbs. butter
1/4 cup milk or cream

Sprinkle oysters with salt and pepper. Roll in cracker crumbs. Beat 1 egg well. Dip cracker covered oysters in egg. Roll in cracker crumbs again. Melt butter in large frying pan. Add oysters and brown lightly, 2 to 4 minutes. Beat remaining eggs with milk. Season with salt and pepper. Pour eggs into frying pan. Cook eggs and oysters slowly, over low heat, until eggs are set. When done, slide onto a serving platter and fold in half. Makes 4 servings.

SCALONE

You'll need a food processor or meat grinder to prepare this recipe. What's nice is that you don't have to tenderize the abalone before cooking, because it is ground.

1 lb. abalone
1 lb. sea scallops
1 egg, beaten
1 tsp. salt
2 tbs. oil
2 tbs. butter
flour
lemon slices (optional)

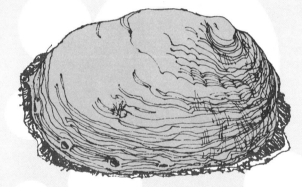

Cube abalone. Put into food processor. Process until well ground. Remove abalone. Add scallops to processor and grind well. Combine abalone, scallops, egg and salt. Shape into flat patties. In a skillet, heat oil and butter. Dip patties in flour. Shake off excess. Fry quickly, a minute or less, per side. If desired, serve with lemon slices. Makes 6 servings.

LOBSTER OR SEAFOOD NEWBURG

This is a delicious way to use leftover lobster, shrimp, crab or scallops.

4 tbs. butter
2 cups diced, cooked lobster, shrimp, crab or scallops
1/4 cup dry sherry
1/2 tsp. paprika
dash of nutmeg
3 egg yolks, beaten
1 cup cream or milk
salt and white pepper to taste
4 large puff pastry shells (from your grocer's frozen foods department),
     or 8 slices toast, buttered

In top of double boiler, melt butter. Stir in lobster. Cook until warm, about 3 minutes. Add sherry. Cook 2 minutes. Add paprika and nutmeg. Over medium heat, add egg yolks and cream. Stir constantly until thickened. Add salt and pepper. Fill pastry shells, or pour over toast. Makes 4 servings.

PAELLA

Of Spanish origin, Paella is distinguished by its saffron flavored rice. Saffron, which is made from the dried stamens of a cultivated crocus, primarily grown in Spain, is very expensive. It takes hundreds of thousands of these stamens to produce one ounce of saffron powder. You can buy it in 3/64ths of an ounce increments at a gourmet foods store. The superb "old world" flavor that it imparts to Paella cannot be achieved by the substitution of any other spice.

A spectacular dish to serve company. Traditionally served in a Paellero, a large, round, shallow dish about fifteen inches in diameter which can be purchased at a cookware store. Or, you may substitute any large, shallow oven-proof dish of your own.

1/4 cup olive oil
6 **each,** chicken drumsticks and thighs
3 whole chicken breasts, split into 4 pieces each
1/2 lb. chorizo or hot Italian sausage, cut into 2-inch chunks
2 cups long grain rice
3/4 cup sliced green onion, with green tops
4 cloves garlic, minced
2 stalks celery, chopped
1 green pepper, seeded and chopped
1 tsp. saffron
1 tsp. salt
1 tsp. oregano
4 cups chicken stock
1 can (15 ozs.) artichoke hearts, halved
20 large fresh shrimp, shelled and deveined (see page 48)
20 fresh clams, in their shells, well scrubbed

124

Heat olive oil in frying pan over medium-high heat. Add chicken pieces, and brown thoroughly. Remove chicken and drain well on paper towels. Add chorizo, brown well. Remove and drain on paper towels. Drain all but 1/4-cup of fat. Add rice, onion, garlic, celery and green pepper. Saute over medium heat, until rice is golden and vegetables are somewhat soft. Add saffron, salt, oregano, stock and artichoke hearts. Simmer for five minutes. Pour rice mixture into one or more large, shallow baking dishes. Rice should be no closer than one inch to the top of the dish. Arrange chicken pieces attractively on top of the rice. Cover, with lid or aluminum foil, and bake at 350°F. for 20 minutes. Arrange raw shrimp and clams on top of rice mixture. Cover and bake for an additional 8 minutes. Makes 8 to 10 servings.

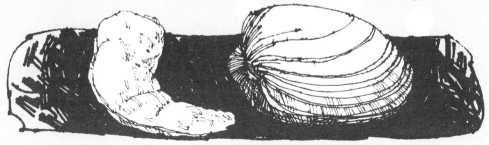

LINGUINE WITH CLAM SAUCE

Absolutely spectacular with fresh clams and homemade noodles.

1/4 cup butter
3 cloves garlic, minced
1/2 cup heavy cream
salt and pepper to taste
20 to 24 fresh, clams, steamed and shucked (see page 36), with liquor reserved,
    or 1 can (8 ozs.) clams
linguine noodles to serve 4
1/2 cup grated Parmesan cheese

Melt butter in saucepan over medium-low heat. Add garlic. Saute for 5 to 8 minutes. Watch carefully, so that butter does not burn. Add cream, salt, pepper and reserved clam liquor. Keep mixture warm over low heat. Boil noodles until done. Drain. Add clams to cream mixture. Heat until just warm. Divide noodles among plates. Top with clam sauce. Sprinkle with cheese. Makes 4 servings.

HERB FRIED SCALLOPS

Crisp on the outside, tender in the middle. These delicate morsels will melt in your mouth

1 lb. ocean scallops
2 eggs
1 tbs. lemon juice
1 cup fine dry bread crumbs
1/2 tsp. dried herbs (thyme, tarragon, dill and parsley)
vegetable oil
Tartar Sauce

Clean and rinse scallops. Cut large ones in half. Dry completely on paper towels. Beat eggs well. Add lemon juice. Mix your choice of herbs with bread crumbs. Dip scallops in crumbs, in egg mixture, then in crumbs again. Heat 1/4-inch of oil in frying pan. Fry coated scallops about 3 minutes on each side, until golden. Drain on paper towels. Serve immediately with Tartar Sauce. Makes 4 servings.

COQUILLES ST. JACQUES

This is a classic.

1-1/2 lbs. fresh or frozen scallops
3/4 cup dry white wine **or** chicken broth
1 bay leaf
1/2 tsp. salt
1-1/2 cups thinly sliced fresh mushrooms
2 tbs. green onion
1/4 cup butter
6 tbs. flour
dash white pepper
1/4 tsp. nutmeg
1 cup light cream
2 tbs. butter, melted
1 cup soft bread crumbs

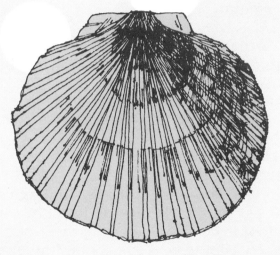

Thaw scallops, if frozen. Place in saucepan with wine and bay leaf. Simmer about

2 minutes, until scallops turn white. Remove scallops. Pour wine poaching liquid from saucepan into measuring cup. Add enough broth to liquid to bring the two up to the one cup mark. Saute mushrooms and onions in 1/4 cup butter until tender. Stir in flour, pepper and nutmeg. Blend until flour is absorbed. Add reserved poaching liquid and cream. Stir until thick. Add scallops. Warm over low heat. Do not boil, or mixture will curdle and scallops will toughen. Butter 6 baking shells, ramekins, or custard cups (6 ozs.). Divide mixture evenly among containers and fill. Add bread crumbs to remaining 2 tablespoons of butter. Sprinkle over top of scallop mixture. Bake at 400°F. about 5 to 7 minutes, until lightly browned.

SOUP

There are many different names for soup, especially when you're talking about seafood soup. Fish stock is the most clear of all seafood soups. It is identical to broth, consomme and bouillon in consistency. And, like these soups, it is used as a "base" in sauces, main dishes and stew soups. Chowder is a combination of fish or shellfish, vegetables, herbs, spices and, usually, milk or cream. Bisque contains more cream than chowder, and is therefore more rich. Only shellfish are used in bisque. The most hearty and filling of all seafood soups are gumbos and seafood stews. Gumbo, which originated in the south, is distinguished by its file powder. File, often called file gumbo, is a spice and thickening agent introduced to the Creoles of New Orleans by native indians. Most gumbos and seafood stews, such as bouillabaisse, consist of a mixture of fish and shellfish in a rather spicy, thin tomato based broth.

While the best meat soups are made after long hours of slow cooking, this is definitely not the case with seafood soups. Even the fish stock, on which the most hearty seafood stews are based, needs only minimal cooking. You might simmer the tomato broth of a stew for an hour or so, but don't add the seafood until the last few minutes of cooking.

Any of these soups may be served as an appetizer, first course or main dish.

QUICK FISH STOCK

Avoid using strong-flavored fish such as mackerel, bluefish or skate.

1 fresh, medium-sized uncooked fish skeleton and head
1 tsp. salt
1/4 cup vinegar

Scrape as much flesh from skeleton as possible. Poach in 4 cups of boiling water, salt and vinegar for 1 minute. Remove bones. Cool. Reserve liquid. If there is any flesh on the skeleton, pull it off and reserve it. Return bones to liquid. Simmer for 15 minutes. Discard skeleton. Strain liquid. Return fish pieces to liquid. Refrigerate and use within three days. May be frozen in air tight containers up to 6 months. Makes about 4 cups.

COURT BOUILLON

Court bouillon is a flavored liquid in which fish can be poached.

2 qts. water
1 cup dry white wine
1/2 cup white **or** tarragon vinegar
2 stalks celery, chopped
2 carrots, chopped
1 onion stuck with 5 cloves
1 sprig dill
1 tsp. **each** tarragon, chives, thyme, chervil **or** parsley
4 whole peppercorns
1 tbs. salt

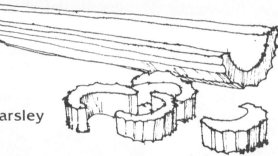

Combine all ingredients and simmer for 30 minutes. May be used immediately or strained and refrigerated for a few days. Double or triple recipe as needed. Makes 2 quarts.

SCALLOP SOUP

The coriander in this easy soup has a slightly oriental flavor.

4 cups chicken broth
1/3 lb. scallops, thoroughly defrosted, if frozen
1 egg, slightly beaten
16 very thin (julienne) slices of ham, about 3 inches long and 1/4 inch wide
1 tsp. coriander

Place broth over medium heat and simmer. In a separate saucepan, place scallops over, not in, boiling water, in a steamer. Steam for 3 to 4 minutes, until just done. Remove scallops and slice them very thinly. Remove broth from heat. In a thin, steady stream, stir egg into broth. Add scallops. Pour soup into 4 soup bowls. Garnish with ham and coriander. Makes 4 servings.

 # MANHATTAN CLAM CHOWDER

1 pint clams, **or** 2 cans, 8 ozs. each
4 strips bacon, diced
1/2 cup chopped onion
1/2 cup chopped celery
1/4 cup chopped green pepper
2 cups diced potatoes

1/4 tsp. sage
1/4 tsp. thyme
1-1/2 tsp. salt
dash cayenne
3 cups canned tomatoes,
    crushed, with juice

Drain clams, reserving liquor. Chop coarsely. Fry bacon over medium heat until it renders most of its fat. Don't let it become crispy. Add onion, celery and green pepper. Cook about 5 minutes, or until tender. Add clam liquor to measuring cup. Add enough water to equal one cup. Add potatoes and seasonings. Cook 15 to 20 minutes, until potatoes are tender. Add clams and tomatoes with juice. Heat until just warm. Makes 6 servings.

BOUILLABAISSE

2 lbs. fin fish (red snapper, haddock, flounder, rock **or** sea trout, **or** combination)
1/2 to 1 lb. shrimp, lobster, scallops, crabmeat, **or** combination
18 small clams, mussels, oysters, **or** lobster claws, in their shells
1/4 cup olive oil
1 large onion, finely chopped

2 shallots, minced
4 cloves garlic, minced
2 cups fish stock, clam juice, **or** chicken broth
1 can (13 ozs.) tomatoes with liquid
2 tsp. salt
dash cayenne
1/2 tsp. **each** thyme, basil and saffron
chopped parsley (optional)

Cut fish into bite-sized pieces. Shell shrimp, lobster or crab if desired. (Traditionalists prefer to leave the shells on during the cooking process. They believe it gives the stew a better flavor.) Scrub clams, mussels, oysters or lobster claws well. Heat oil. Saute onions, shallots and garlic about 10 minutes. Add liquid, tomatoes and seasonings, except parsley. Lower heat and simmer 15 minutes. Add all seafood. Cover and cook 10 minutes. Discard any clams that have not opened. Serve in large bowls, sprinkled generously with parsley. Makes 6 servings.

NEW ENGLAND CLAM CHOWDER

30 fresh chowder clams, **or** 2 cups canned clams
4 slices bacon, diced
1/2 cup diced onions
1/2 cup chopped celery
4 medium potatoes, peeled and diced
water

2 cups light cream
salt and pepper to taste
1/2 tsp. oregano
1/8 tsp. marjoram
1/4 tsp. thyme

If you are using fresh clams, shuck them (see page 36). Reserve the liquor, or juice, from each clam. If you are using canned clams, drain them and reserve their liquor also. Chop clams coarsely. Fry bacon in skillet until crisp. Remove from pan and drain on paper towels. Reduce heat in pan, add onions to bacon grease, and fry until tender. Add celery. Cook for 3 minutes more. Add potatoes, reserved liquor and enough water to cover potatoes. Simmer for 25 to 30 minutes, or until potatoes are tender. Add clams and cook for 3 minutes. Reduce heat to low and slowly add cream, bacon, salt, pepper, oregano, marjoram and thyme. Heat until just warm. Do not boil, or cream will curdle. Makes 8 servings.

OYSTER STEW

1 tbs. butter
2 strips bacon, diced
1 tbs. grated onion, **or**
   1 clove garlic, mashed
1/4 cup finely chopped celery
1/4 tsp. Worcestershire sauce

1 to 1-1/2 pints shucked oysters
   (see page 50) with liquor reserved
1-1/2 cups milk
1/2 cup cream
salt and white pepper to taste
chopped parsley or chives (optional)

Melt butter and fry bacon in saucepan over medium heat until bacon renders most of its fat. Add onion and celery. Saute 5 minutes. Add Worcestershire sauce, oysters, oyster liquor, milk, cream, salt and pepper. Stir gently over low heat until oysters float and mixture is hot. If desired, sprinkle with parsley. Serve immediately. Makes about 4 cups.

LOBSTER BISQUE

2 medium-sized lobsters, broiled (see page 41)
3 cups Quick Fish Stock, page 132
1 medium onion, quartered
4 celery stalks, with leaves
2 whole cloves
1 large bay leaf
7 peppercorns
1/4 cup butter

1/4 cup flour
3 cups warm milk
1/4 tsp. nutmeg
3/4 cup warm cream
salt and white pepper to taste
minced parsley (optional)
paprika (optional)

Remove meat from lobster and dice. Reserve. Crush shells and add them to a large soup kettle along with Fish Stock, onion, celery, cloves, bay leaf and peppercorns. Simmer for 30 minutes. Strain stock. Reserve liquid. Melt butter over medium heat. Gradually stir in flour. Let roux bubble 30 seconds. Add milk and nutmeg. Stir constantly until smooth. Add lobster and stock. Simmer bisque covered for 5 minutes. Remove kettle from heat. Stir in cream, salt and pepper. Serve immediately sprinkled with parsley and paprika, if desired. Makes about 8 cups.

SEAFOOD SOUP IN A HURRY

If you have some leftover flatfish, shrimp and lobster, prepare this soup for dinner. No one will ever suspect they are eating leftovers!

1/4 cup butter
1-1/2 cups cooked flatfish fillets, chopped
1 cup white wine
3/4 cup cooked shrimp, shelled and
    deveined (see page 48)
3/4 cup chopped, cooked lobster meat
1 small can sliced mushrooms

1 can condensed cream of chicken soup
1 tbs. chopped canned pimentos
2 cloves garlic, crushed
1/2 tsp. paprika
1/2 cup sherry (optional)
salt and white pepper to taste

Melt butter over medium heat in a large saucepan. Add rest of ingredients, except sherry, salt and pepper. Simmer over low heat 10 minutes. Add sherry, salt and pepper. Makes 4 servings.

SEAFOOD GUMBO A LA BUNDY

There are many versions of Gumbo. The traditional, southern method uses a roux (a "paste") made from oil and flour. This produces a somewhat heavy flavor, which many non-southerners are not used to. For a lighter taste, use butter instead of oil. The Commander's Palace, a fine restaurant in New Orleans, uses no roux at all. The chef there prefers a simple seafood broth. You should be able to find gumbo file at almost any gourmet foods store.

2 lbs. fresh crabmeat
1 lb. raw shrimp
1 pint shucked oysters (see page 50)
3/4 cup oil or butter
2/3 cup flour
1 cup chopped onion
4 cloves of garlic, minced
1 can (16 ozs.) tomatoes, chopped
1 bay leaf

1 tsp. chopped parsley
1-1/2 tsp. salt
1 sprig thyme (or 1/8 tsp. ground)
1 hot pepper pod, **or** dash cayenne
1-1/2 lbs. fresh okra, sliced **or**, 2 pkg. frozen sliced okra
1/4 tsp. gumbo file powder, **or** more boiled rice to serve 10

Pick out and discard any cartilage in crabmeat. Shell and devein shrimp (see page 48). Drain oysters and reserve their liquor. In a large soup kettle, bring 3 quarts of water to a boil. In a separate pan, heat oil or melt butter. Add flour. Heat until mixture bubbles. If you are using oil, mixture must turn a dark brown. Do not let it burn, however. Add onions and garlic. Cook over low heat 4 minutes. Add roux to boiling water. Add tomatoes, bay leaf, parsley, salt, thyme, pepper, okra and oyster liquor. Simmer over very low heat at least 2 hours. Gumbo may be prepared up to this point a day in advance. 20 minutes before serving, add seafood. 5 minutes before serving, add gumbo file. Serve in warm soup bowls over rice. Makes 10 servings.

CIOPPINO

This popular West Coast dish of crab, shrimp, clams and fish is ideal for informal entertaining. Provide each guest with a large bib. Serve with lots of crusty French bread, a tossed salad, and a fresh fruit for dessert. You may vary the fish according to what your local market offers.

1/4 cup olive oil
1 medium onion, chopped
4 stalks celery, thinly sliced
4 medium carrots, thinly sliced
8 cloves garlic, minced
1/4 cup chopped parsley
1 can (1 lb. 12 ozs.) solid pack tomatoes,
    or 4 large, fresh tomatoes, chopped
2 cans (8 ozs. each) tomato sauce
1-1/2 cups water or clam juice, or combination
1 cup dry sherry
1 lemon, thinly sliced

144

1-1/2 tsp. **each** sweet basil, marjoram, oregano and thyme
salt and pepper to taste
1-1/2 lb. firm, white fish, cut into bite-sized pieces (flounder, turbot, halibut)
1 lb. raw prawns or shrimp, in shell
2 lbs. clams in shell, well scrubbed
1 or 2 Dungeness, or 4 to 6 blue crabs, cooked, cleaned and cracked (see page 38)

Heat oil in large kettle or Dutch oven. Add vegetables. Saute until tender, about 10 minutes. Add remaining ingredients, except fish and shellfish. Simmer gently 1-1/2 hours. The broth will have the best flavor if it is prepared one day in advance. 20 minutes before serving, add fish and shellfish to simmering broth. Cover and cook 20 minutes. Discard any clams that have not opened. To serve, ladle some of each kind of fish into warm soup bowls. Top with broth. Make it easy on your family or guests and serve extra bowls to discard shells in. Finger bowls, in which to wash your hands, would be nice also. Makes 8 servings.

SALADS

When it's hot outside and you don't feel like cooking, why not put together a seafood salad? These recipes are quick and easy to prepare. Many of them can be assembled the day before you plan on serving them.

Seafood salads are a natural for dieters or people just trying to "eat light." The low-calorie protein found in seafood, coupled with the vitamins found in the other vegetables or fruits, make seafood salads a well rounded meal.

When you are serving seafood salads, make sure all the ingredients are the freshest possible. Nothing is worse than limp lettuce. For really perfect salads, chill the salad plates and forks. To make your salad lovely to look at as well as delicious, add one of the Garnishes for Fish suggested on page 153.

CHINESE SEAFOOD SALAD

Prepare the salad and dressing the day before. Add the fried noodles just before serving. To stretch for 10 to 12 servings, add more pineapple and a larger can of noodles.

1 can (6 ozs.) crab, drained
1 can (4-1/2 ozs.) shrimp, drained
4 eggs, hard boiled and sliced
3/4 cup celery, chopped
1/4 cup chopped green pepper
1/2 cup sliced green onions with tops

1 can (8-1/4 ozs.) pineapple cubes, drained
1 cup mayonnaise
1/4 cup red wine vinegar
1 can (3 ozs.) fried Chow Mein noodles,
    or rice noodles
lettuce

Remove any cartilage from crabmeat. Mix crab, shrimp, eggs, celery, green pepper, onions and pineapple. Mix together mayonnaise and vinegar. Pour over crab mixture. Refrigerate overnight. Just before serving add noodles and toss gently. Serve on lettuce leaves. Makes 8 servings.

HAOLE LOMI-LOMI

This Hawaiian salad is really a crowd pleaser. Any firm fish can be substituted for the salmon. Perfect for a buffet.

Simple Court Bouillon
5 lbs. fresh salmon
3 cups sliced green onions with tops
8 medium-sized tomatoes, chopped
salt to taste
freshly ground pepper

Simple Court Bouillon:
2 qts. water **plus** 4 tbs. salt
2 lemons, sliced
3 tbs. lemon juice
2 bay leaves
12 whole peppercorns

In a fish poacher, or pan suitable to poach fish in, pour 2 quarts of water and add all the ingredients for Simple Court Bouillon. Place fish in poacher. Cook about 12 minutes, or until fish flakes. Remove pan from heat. Cool fish and bouillon in refrigerator. When cold remove from liquid. Skin, debone and flake salmon. Refrigerate until serving time. Just before serving, combine salmon, onions, tomatoes, salt and pepper. Serve in a large bowl. Makes 12 salads.

JACK'S STUFFED ARTICHOKES

My friend Jack, who has a knack in the kitchen, created this delectable recipe.

4 medium-sized artichokes, **or** 2 large avocados
2 tbs. vegetables oil
1-1/2 tbs. vinegar
1 clove garlic, mashed
juice of 1 lemon

1-1/2 cups fresh shrimp, crab or
   scallops cooked and chilled
1 cup, or more, mayonnaise
1/2 tsp. curry (optional)
dash cayenne pepper

Core artichokes, making sure to completely remove the stringy "choke." If desired, snip off the prickly ends of the leaves. Cut off stem, so that artichoke can stand on a flat surface. In a large kettle, or Dutch oven, bring 2 quarts of water, oil, vinegar and garlic to a boil. Drop in artichokes. Reduce heat to medium. Cook about 45 minutes, or until fork pierces stem easily. Remove from water. Drain well. Chill until cold. If using avocados, peel, slice once lengthwise and remove seed. Drizzle lemon juice over avocado to prevent it from turning brown. Set aside. Combine shrimp, mayonnaise, curry and cayenne. Chill until cold. Stuff artichokes or avocados with shrimp mixture. Makes 4 servings.

CURRIED SHRIMP AND MELON SALAD

A marvelous luncheon or light supper dish. Use any melon in season.

2 lbs. fresh shrimp
3/4 cup mayonnaise
1/4 cup sour cream
2 tbs. sliced green onion
2 tbs. lemon juice
1-1/2 cups chopped celery
4 to 5 tsp. curry powder

2 medium-sized honeydew melons
2/3 cup oil
1/3 cup lemon juice
salad greens
Condiments: crisp bacon bits, chopped cashews,
   or peanuts, shredded coconut, chutney

Cook and clean the shrimp (see page 48). Set aside. Combine mayonnaise, sour cream, onion, lemon juice, celery and curry powder. Add shrimp. Chill several hours, or overnight. Halve and seed melons. Make balls. Reserve melon shells. Toss balls lightly with oil and lemon juice. Chill. Lightly salt melon halves and turn upside down to drain. Chill. Just before serving cut off a slice of bottom of melon to make it more stable. Fill melons with shrimp mixture. Garnish with drained melon balls. Place on greens on salad plates. Pass condiments. Makes 4 servings.

GARNISHES FOR FISH

Compliment any seafood dish with a garnish. By adding one or more of the following vegetables or fruits you will not only perk up that dish, but also make it look more "professional."

To add GREEN: Avocado slices; celery tops, sticks or curls; chopped chives or green onion tops; cucumber spears or round slices; curly endive; dill sprigs; green peppers cut into sticks or rings; lettuce; lime slices, twists or wedges; mint sprigs; green or stuffed olives; pickles.

To add RED: Beets; cranberry sauce; paprika; pimentos; radishes; spiced crab apples; tomatoes.

To add YELLOW/ORANGE: Carrot sticks, curls or shreds; grapefruit sections; hard boiled egg yolks; melon balls; peaches; pineapple.

Other ideas: Black olives; fluted mushrooms; grape clusters; toasted nuts.

CRAB OR SHRIMP LOUIE

On the West Coast, this is a favorite way to serve cold crab.

1 large Dungeness crab, cooked and cleaned,
   or 2 cups small shrimp, cooked and deveined
   (see page 38)
1 cup mayonnaise
2 tbs. chopped parsley
2 tbs. chili sauce
1 tbs. catsup

1 tsp. Worcestershire sauce
1 tsp. A-1 steak sauce
lettuce
endive
tomato wedges
hard boiled eggs

Crack crab and pick out meat. Combine mayonnaise, parsley, chili sauce, catsup, Worcestershire sauce and A-1. Arrange lettuce and endive on chilled salad plates. Spoon crab over greens. Add tomato wedges. Spoon sauce over top. Garnish with slices or wedges of hard cooked eggs. Makes 4 servings.

CITRUS SEAFOOD SALAD

Any firm white fish, local to your area, may be used in this recipe. Shrimp is also delicious prepared this way.

2 cups fresh fish fillets,
   or 2 cups cooked and cleaned shrimp
2 grapefruits, peeled, cored and sectioned
2 oranges, peeled, cored and sectioned
1/4 cup chopped green onions, with tops
salad greens
1/2 ripe avocado, peeled and sliced

Salad Dressing:
1/4 cup **each** vinegar, oil and catsup
2 tbs. sugar
1 tsp. chili powder
1 clove garlic, mashed

Poach fish in simmering, salted water for 8 to 10 minutes. Cool in liquid. When cold, remove from liquid and debone. Chill. Mix together grapefruit and orange sections. Add onion. Chill. Combine all ingredients for salad dressing. Just before serving, combine fish with fruit mixture. Moisten with salad dressing. Arrange greens on plates. Scoop salad onto greens. Garnish with avocado slices. Makes 4 servings.

HERRING POTATO SALAD

A pleasant change from ordinary potato salad.

2 cups diced, boiled potatoes
1 cup diced, pickled herring fillets
3/4 cup chopped celery, with leaves
1 tbs. minced parsley
1 tbs. minced chives
1/3 cup sour cream
1-1/2 tbs. lemon juice
1/2 tsp. paprika
lettuce leaves to serve 6

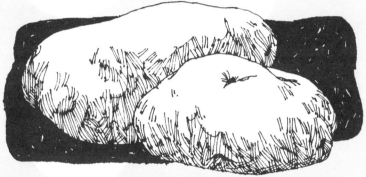

Combine all ingredients except lettuce leaves, and toss gently. Arrange lettuce leaves on chilled salad plates. Spoon salad onto lettuce. Makes 6 servings.

156

ICELANDIC TROUT SALAD

You will have to visit a gourmet shop or large department store in order to purchase the main ingredient in this salad. Iceland Brook Trout is canned by the ORA Food Processing Company, Ltd. in Reykjavik, Iceland. The tiny fish are packed six to a tin. They can be eaten whole. But, I prefer to remove the bones.

2 cans (10 ozs. each) Iceland Brook Trout
shredded lettuce and spinach
2 tbs. finely minced green onion
1/2 cup ripe avocado, cut into small pieces

2 hard boiled eggs, quartered
Horseradish Sauce, page 168
4 thin slices lemon (optional)
capers (optional)

Drain liquid from trout. Arrange a bed of lettuce and spinach on four plates. Place trout on greens. Sprinkle with onion, celery and avocado. Place two egg quarters on each plate. Spoon Horseradish Sauce over top. Cut lemon to form twist. Garnish with lemon and capers. Makes 4 servings.

SEAFOOD MOUSSE

Want to impress your guests at your next party? Pour this mousse into a fish mold. Turn it out onto a large platter lined with lettuce. A super spectacular!

1-1/2 cups crab, lobster **or** tuna,
   or any combination of these
1 cup finely chopped celery
1/2 cup finely chopped green pepper /
   or cucumber
1/4 cup finely chopped green onion,
   with tops
1 tsp. salt
1/4 cup lemon juice

1 tbs. Worcestershire sauce
1 can (10-1/2 ozs.) tomato soup, undiluted
1 small pkg. (3-1/2 ozs.) cream cheese
3 envelopes unflavored gelatin
1 cup cold water
1 cup mayonnaise
lettuce, enough for large platter
tomato wedges, for garnish
cucumber slices, for garnish

Drain and flake seafood. Combine with celery, green pepper, onion, salt, lemon juice and Worcestershire sauce. In the top of a double boiler, mix together soup and cream cheese. Simmer over water until cheese melts. Soften gelatin in cold water.

Add gelatin to soup mixture. Simmer over water until gelatin dissolves. Cool. Stir in mayonnaise and seafood mixture. Spoon into a 1-1/2-quart fish or ring mold. Chill several hours, until firm. Just before serving, dip mold briefly in hot water, to loosen. Invert onto platter that has been lined with lettuce. Garnish with tomatoes and cucumber slices. Makes 8 servings.

SAUCES

If you live in an area which has a narrow selection of seafood, don't despair. A good repertoire of sauces, like the ones contained in this chapter, will help you avoid boredom. A simple Herb Butter Sauce, which can be prepared in minutes, will perk up any baked, broiled or fried fish. My Quick Hollandaise Sauce, which is practically failure-proof, can be poured over almost any seafood. It is impressive enough to serve to your dinner guests, but easy enough to make for yourself any night of the week.

The most important thing to remember when you are planning to serve a sauce with your seafood is this: The sauce should enhance, rather than cover up, the flavor of the seafood. Delicate seafoods need only subtle enhancement, such as, my Green or Cucumber Sauces will give. More flavorful seafood, with darker colored meat, go well with such sauces as Horseradish and Danish Mustard.

 **BASTING SAUCE**

A delightful piquant sauce used for basting your favorite pan fried, broiled or baked fish.

4 tbs. butter, melted
4 tbs. lemon juice
4 tbs. catsup
1/2 tsp. seafood seasoning
1/2 tsp. salt

Mix all ingredients. Makes 3/4 cup.

SEAFOOD COCKTAIL SAUCE

A perfect "topper" for any fresh shellfish.

1/2 cup ketchup **or** chili sauce
1 tbs. diced onion
2 tbs. lemon juice
2 tsp. horseradish

1 tsp. Worcestershire sauce
dash Tabasco sauce, if desired
salt to taste

Combine all ingredients. Chill at least 1 hour before serving. Makes 4 servings.

MUSTARD SAUCE

Serve with any fried seafood.

1/2 cup mayonnaise
1 tbs. Dijon mustard

1 tbs. vinegar

Combine ingredients. Makes 1/2 cup.

163

GREEN SAUCE

A superb dip for cooked scallops or shrimp. Also good over salmon or swordfish steaks.

1 cup mayonnaise
1/4 cup minced parsley
1/4 cup minced chives **or** green onion tops
1/2 cup finely minced spinach
1/2 tsp. dill

Mix all ingredients. Chill to blend flavors. Makes 2 cups.

CUCUMBER SAUCE

Especially good for cold fish.

3 large cucumbers
2 tsp. salt
1 cup sour cream **or** unflavored yogurt
1 cup mayonnaise
1 tbs. vinegar
1/2 tsp. dill
dash garlic powder

Peel and halve cucumbers. Scoop out seeds. Chop finely. Place in bowl with salt. Cover with a weight, such as a small plate. Chill at least two hours. Drain. Add remaining ingredients. Mix thoroughly. Chill. Makes 3-1/2 cups.

165

 ## QUICK HOLLANDAISE SAUCE

When you are in a hurry this is a great recipe to remember. It is the perfect embellishment for many fish. It is somewhat lighter and fluffier than the traditional version.

1/2 cup butter (1 stick)
3 egg yolks
1 tbs. lemon juice
1/4 tsp. salt
1/4 tsp. dry mustard
pinch cayenne pepper

Heat butter to bubbling in a small pan. Watch carefully. Don't allow to burn. Place egg yolks, lemon juice, salt, mustard and pepper in blender. Cover and turn on low speed for three seconds. With blender still operating remove cover and add bubbling butter in a steady stream. When all has been added, turn off blender. Serve immediately or keep warm over hot water. Makes about 1 cup.

REMOULADE SAUCE

The perfect accompaniment for cold cooked shrimp or poached scallops. For the best flavor, pour the sauce over hot shellfish and allow it to cool before chilling.

2 tbs. Dijon mustard
1 tbs. catsup
1 tsp. paprika
1/2 tsp. salt
1/4 tsp. cayenne pepper
1 tbs. lemon juice

1/4 cup tarragon vinegar
1/2 cup salad oil
1/4 cup chopped celery
1/4 cup chopped green onion
1 tbs. chopped parsley
1 tsp. finely chopped capers

Mix mustard, catsup, paprika, salt, pepper and lemon juice. Stir in vinegar. Slowly add oil. Add remaining ingredients. Refrigerate several hours before using to allow flavors to blend. Makes 1-1/2 cups.

HORSERADISH SAUCE

A very versatille sauce that's great with seafood, ham and roast beef

1 cup whipping cream
1/2 tsp. salt
1/2 tsp. white pepper
2 to 3 tbs. ground horseradish
2 tbs. white vinegar
2 tsp. sugar

Whip cream. Fold in remaining ingredients. Chill at least 1 hour to blend flavors. Makes about 1-1/4 cups.

HERB BUTTER SAUCE

Any mild fish will be enhanced with this herb sauce.

3 tbs. tarragon vinegar
2 tsp. chopped shallots
1/4 cup butter
1 tbs. chopped chives
1 tbs. chopped chervil **or** parsley
1/4 tsp. thyme
1/8 tsp. fennel seed

Combine vinegar and shallots in a saucepan. Bring to a boil. Add remaining ingredients. Pour over cooked fish. Makes 1/2 cup.

INDEX

173

174

Main Dishes

For Fish:

181